The Chalet Girls Cook Book

Elinor M Brent-Dyer

Girls Gone By Publishers

COMPLETE AND UNABRIDGED

Published by Girls Gone By Publishers, 4 Rock Terrace, Coleford, Bath, Somerset BA3 5NF

First published by W & R Chambers Ltd 1953
This edition published 2009
Text and Chalet School characters © Girls Gone By Publishers
Introduction © Ruth Jolly and Adrianne Fitzpatrick 2009
The First Appearance of *The Chalet Girls' Cook Book*: A Publishing History © Clarissa Cridland 2009
"Cooking the Book" & photographs © Ruth Jolly and Adrianne Fitzpatrick 2009
Appendix: Recipes from *The Third Chalet Book for Girls* © Girls Gone By Publishers
Errors in the First Edition © Ruth Jolly and Alison Neale 2009
Discovering the Chalet School Series © Clarissa Cridland 2002
Elinor M Brent-Dyer: a Brief Biography © Clarissa Cridland 2002
Design and Layout © Girls Gone By Publishers 2009

All rights reserved. Without limiting the rights under copyright reserved above, no part of this publication may be reproduced, stored in or introduced into a retrieval system, or transmitted, in any form or by any means (electronic, mechanical, photocopying, recording or otherwise), without the prior written permission of the above copyright owners and the above publisher of this book.

Typeset in England by AJF   Cover design by Ken Websdale
Printed in England by CPI Antony Rowe

ISBN 978-1-84745-078-4

CONTENTS

Introduction	5
The First Appearance of *The Chalet Girls' Cook Book*: A Publishing History	13
The Chalet Girls' Cook Book	19
Cooking the Book	183
Errors in the First Edition	206
Appendix: Recipes from *The Third Chalet Book for Girls*	208
Discovering the Chalet School Series	210
Elinor M Brent-Dyer: a Brief Biography	215
Complete Numerical List of Titles (Chambers and Girls Gone By)	217
Complete Numerical List of Titles (Armada/Collins)	220
New Chalet School Titles	222
Further Reading	224
Index of Recipes	225

INTRODUCTION

Research into nutrition is constantly advancing, and one generation's cherished belief is another generation's anathema. We do not necessarily subscribe to the Quartette's views on what constitutes a healthy menu, and would advise readers to follow best practice as understood in their own culture and generation.

The Chalet Girls' Cook Book was published in 1953, but parts of it date from the 1940s, and the whole approach to cooking and recipes belongs to an era far removed from the present day. All the measurements in this book are imperial, and oven temperatures are in Fahrenheit, with an occasional gas regulo as an alternative. Assumptions about cooking methods and styles of eating have changed, and the modern reader may require some interpretation to get the best out of the book. This introduction provides a few explanations which may be useful, and in our postscript article "Cooking the Book" we give an account of our own experience of following Elinor Brent-Dyer's directions.

There were some things mentioned by EBD, both ingredients and techniques, with which we ourselves were not familiar, and some which struck us as being distinctly unusual. We had not heard, for example, of Vienna flour, but a little research threw up the information that it is a specially fine flour used to make strudel pastry, Vienna bread, and cakes; in fact, premium white flour. Apparently in the USA it is known as pastry flour.

The concept of "oiling" butter was new to us as well, and we did wonder at first if it was a misprint for "boiling", but it turned out to mean "reaching an oily consistency" when heated or melted—the dictionary informed us that it is now a rare usage, but not obsolete. On the other hand, we found nothing to explain what Simone means by her instruction to "fire" a cake tin: perhaps she means "fill", but we could not be sure, so we left it unchanged.

One thing we find ourselves unable to accept, though, is EBD's description of soy sauce. "It is just Béchamel sauce, only made with soya bean flour instead of with ordinary flour," explains Frieda; but no one who had ever eaten Chop Suey (the recipe for which it is listed) could make such a statement, and we can only conclude that EBD had not. Her assumption is not in itself ridiculous, however: we did come across a recipe for white sauce which used soya flour in lieu of wheat flour, and she might have had such a recipe and have jumped to a conclusion.

Another occasion when we wondered if she had actually tried what she was recommending arose when we read the instructions for fried rice. Nowhere is it mentioned that the rice should be pre-cooked, or—on the paella method—that it must be simmered with stock after frying. We wondered what would happen if it wasn't …

We were intrigued by Jo's question: "Do you mean *two*-gills-one-pint, or *four*-gills-one-pint?"— Ruth in particular remembers chanting her tables at primary school, and it was definitely four gills to the pint. Adrianne, however, came up with a reference which stated that as a pub measure, the gill was a quarter pint in the south of England but a half pint in the north. EBD came from the north, so would presumably have been familiar with this discrepancy.

It's very interesting to note those ingredients which are viewed by Elinor Brent-Dyer as exotic, or which seem to her to need explanation. The last few decades have seen a great influx of continental recipes into British cooking—the Italian, Spanish and Greek influences have been particularly noticeable, probably because of the availability of cheap holidays in those countries!

When Simone tells us how to cook chips, she remarks: "Oil—olive oil—is the best for this, but you can use lard. Use dripping only if you cannot get either of the others." It is doubtful whether most 21st-century readers would even contemplate using anything other than oil to fry chips. And it is very widely accepted in these days that olive oil is a particularly healthy option, if deep frying can ever be viewed as healthy; although Simone at this point seems to be recommending it on grounds of taste rather than nutrition. Likewise, it seems improbable that many of us would express surprise, as Jo does, over the use of soured cream as an adjunct to bortch, though some would tend to prefer a low-fat yoghurt as an alternative. And in this day and age, it is hard to credit Marie's question, "What exactly *is* curry?", although of course it is plausible enough that it should be Joey, with her family connection with India, who is able to enlighten her. It is, perhaps, a little surprising that Joey—who warns elsewhere of the powerful nature of curry powder—should be recommending a whole ounce (28g) of Madras curry powder here, Madras being towards the hot end of the range.

Probably, too, we would be far less likely in these days to exclaim at the concept of pea-pod soup, since mange tout and sugar snap peas are available in every supermarket. And the same goes for fennel, which can really no longer be counted as a rare ingredient.

Interestingly, the recipes for cakes and sweets have hardly changed at all, though some modern authorities would advise against using up milk which has "turned" in scones, since most milk these days is pasteurised and is soured by different bacteria from untreated milk. We might also hesitate to improve the colour of our icing with a few grains scraped from the washing-blue, as Simone recommends—though Ruth remembers her mother using the "blue-bag" to colour birthday-cake icing in the 1950s. A little research on the invaluable internet, however, brings up the information that Reckitt's blue-bags were made from "synthetic ultramarine and baking soda", which sounds not too scary after all.

A complaint sometimes levelled at *The Chalet Girls' Cook Book* is that the recipes are not always sufficiently specific about quantities and cooking temperatures and times. There may be two explanations for this, the first being that this book falls within a tradition of "narrative" cookery books, a genre to which the best known contributor is probably Elizabeth David. In such books, cooking methods and recipes are embedded in a general narrative giving background information about the region or the people; the writing may be lyrical or humorous, and the level of detail given about methods and ingredients can vary considerably. In her *Book of Mediterranean Food*, for example, when describing the Klephti method of cooking partridges, Elizabeth David goes into great detail about the Greek brigands' cooking techniques, involving "cooking birds and meat wrapped up in paper in a primitively constructed oven … an earthen pot, narrowing at the top … laid on its side in a hollow dug at the edge of a bank of earth, and buried. Underneath the pot the earth is scooped out to make room for a fire of resinous pinewood or charcoal, and this is left slowly burning for 2 or 3 hours." After all these minutiae about the origins of the method, all she tells us about its adaptation for modern use is: "At any rate, partridges with a piece of fat bacon, wrapped in buttered paper, and cooked in a very slow oven are worth trying." No instructions about size or quantities; nothing about what to put them on or in; no clear guidance as to oven temperature; and no timings!

Of course, Joey and Co were writing their recipes down from memory, and it's clear that most were family favourites learned by example rather than from a book, which brings us to the other reason for the rather vague directions in some instances. Experienced cooks often work intuitively, measuring by eye and gauging when a meal is cooked more by experience than by the book. Ruth has a cherished recipe for Yorkshire Curd Cheese Cake, passed on by her grandmother, which perfectly illustrates this. It gives all the ingredients, some with quantities, though the last listed is simply "currants"—to taste, presumably. But the cooking instructions reads simply "Try gas no 7 (425 deg)". In fact Ruth's grandmother cooked on a coke-fired Esse range (similar to an Aga), and the oven temperature would have varied according to how windy it was that day and how recently the stove had been riddled. So the cooking time would have varied too.

Readers should, therefore, feel absolutely no compunction about cross-checking against other recipe books or researching unusual-sounding techniques or ingredients, as well as occasionally deviating from the stated procedure and following their own tried-and-tested methods. After all, we'd do the same with any other cookery book.

Ruth Jolly and Adrianne Fitzpatrick

Fahrenheit	Celsius	Gas Mark	Heat of Oven
225°	110°	¼	Very cool
250	120	½	Very cool
275	140	1	Cool
300	150	2	Cool
325	160	3	Moderate
350	180	4	Moderate
375	190	5	Moderately hot
400	200	6	Moderately hot
425	220	7	Hot
450	230	8	Hot
475	240	9	Very hot

1 teaspoon = 5ml
1 dessertspoon = 10ml
3 teaspoons = 1 tablespoon = 15ml = ½ fl oz
2 tablespoons = 30ml = 1 fl oz
100cc = 105ml = 3½ fl oz

Unit of Measure	Equivalent Measurement	Metric Measurement
1 oz (ounce)	1/16 lb (pound)	30 g (28.35 grams)
2 oz	1/8 lb	55 g
3 oz	3/16 lb	85 g
4 oz	1/4 lb	125 g
8 oz	1/2 lb	240 g
12 oz	3/4 lb	375 g
16 oz	1 lb	454 g
32 oz	2 lbs	907 g
1 kilogram	2.2 lbs/35.2 oz	

Imperial (fl oz/pts)	Metric (ml/L)	US Cups	US Pints
1 fl oz	30ml	⅛	
2 fl oz	60ml	¼	
3 fl oz	90ml		
4 fl oz	120ml	½	¼ US pt
5 fl oz = ¼ pt = gill	150ml		
6 fl oz	180ml	¾	
7 fl oz	210ml		
8 fl oz	240 ml	1	½ US pt
9 fl oz	270ml		
10 fl oz = ½ pt	300ml	1¼	
11 fl oz	330ml		
12 fl oz	360ml	1½	¾ US pt
13 fl oz	390ml		
14 fl oz	420ml	1¾	
15 fl oz = ¾ pt	450ml		
16 fl oz	480ml	2	1 US pt
20 fl oz = 1 pt	600ml	2½	
32 fl oz	960ml	4	1 quart
40 fl oz = 2 pts = 1 quart	1.1 L	5	2½ US pts

THE FIRST APPEARANCE OF *THE CHALET GIRLS' COOK BOOK*
A PUBLISHING HISTORY

The Chalet Girls' Cook Book was first published in 1953, in a landscape format (the width being longer than the height) of about 7 x 5½ inches (178 x 140 mm). The dustwrapper has been reproduced as the front cover of this edition. There was a line drawing on the spine (shown on our back cover), and an illustration on the title page, also shown on our title page, which was a wider version of this, with more detail.

But this was not the first appearance of the *Cook Book*—or at least of parts of it. In the late 1940s, Chambers began to publish some *Books for Girls*, starting with *The Chalet Book for Girls* in 1947. These each contained a long story (*The Mystery at the Chalet School* and then *Tom Tackles the Chalet School*, split over two *Books for Girls*), some short stories, both Chalet School and other, and some articles.

The Chalet Book for Girls has an article, "Cooking in Olden Days", on page 76. This concludes:

> We are now entering upon a new and more enlightened era of cookery. We have the past from which to choose and to learn, the present in which to study and experiment, and the future to restore the high standard which English cooking can once again achieve. We have to avoid the weird and wonderful mixtures of mediaeval and Georgian times and the carelessness of the last thirty years. Cooking is an art, but it is one which should *serve*

life and health, not dominate either. This is one reason why the more casual and elastic meal-times of these days are to be encouraged. They fit in with our work and plans—all to the advantage of good health and good cooking.

Underneath this is the picture below, which shows the full version of the picture used on the title page

and on the spine of *The Chalet Girls' Cook Book*.

Open *The Second Chalet Book for Girls* (1948) at page 119 and you will find "The Chalet Girls' Cookery Book", a long story finishing on page 134. This covers Soups and Fish, which became the first two sections in the full length version. There are very few differences—Cook Book instead of Cookery

Book; one "teaspoon" changed to "tablespoon"; split peas changed to lentils; and a little tightening of one sentence (a few words deleted). However, there are four extra illustrations in the early version which were not used in the full length *Cook Book*, and we have included these in our edition, in their rightful places.

The Third Chalet Book for Girls (1949) is a cookery disappointment. Page 142 is a page of recipes, but none of these appeared in the *Cook Book*. For interest, the recipes are printed as an appendix to this book, on page 208. They are simply recipes, with no conversation between Joey and her friends. It is even possible that these were not written by Elinor—her contracts for the *Books for Girls* covered her for the contributions she made, not for absolutely everything in the books. Unfortunately, we do not know what she didn't write.

There was no *Fourth Chalet Book for Girls*—it is possible that these books did not sell very well, as they were in a larger size, like that of an annual, and Chambers were not publishers of annuals. It seems clear that another book was intended, since Elinor wrote a long story, *The Chalet School and Rosalie*, which Chambers published in 1951 as a paperback. So it may be that she had written more recipes, and that is what led to the publication of this *Cook Book*. But if she had written these for the *Books for Girls*, it is odd that they were not used in *The Third Chalet Book for Girls* and that other recipes were used. We shall probably never know.

The Chalet Girls' Cook Book has never been reprinted until the appearance of this GGBP edition; although the short version, "The Chalet Girls' Cookery Book", was reprinted by GGBP in 2004, in *Elinor M Brent-Dyer's Short Stories* (now out of print). Some stories from *The Chalet Book for Girls* were reprinted in 1970 in *My Treasure Hour Bumper Annual* by Murrays Sales & Service Co, but this was only the stories, and none of the articles. And while *My Treasure Hour Playtime Annual* (also Murrays, 1970) contained a couple of articles as well as stories from *The Second Chalet Book for Girls*, they did not include "The Chalet Girls' Cookery Book". I have never found an equivalent volume for *The Third Chalet Book for Girls*, but I suspect, if it exists, that it did not include the page of recipes.

Clarissa Cridland

Girls Gone By Publishers accept no responsibility for the results obtained by following the recipes in this book.

The Chalet Girls' Cook Book

by

Elinor M. Brent-Dyer

CONTENTS

SOUPS	23
FISH	37
MEATS	51
VEGETABLES	69
CREAMS AND PUDDINGS	89
CAKES, BISCUITS AND SWEETS	113
CHEESE DISHES	139
EGG DISHES	151
DRINKS	161
ODDS AND ENDS	171

SOUPS

SOUPS

"IT'S an idea," said Jo, meditatively sucking the end of her pencil. "I vote we do it. Life's a bit boring just now, anyhow."

"I think it's a very good scheme," agreed Marie von Eschenau.

"So do I," put in Frieda Mensch. "As we are in quarantine for the next four weeks, we might use our time this way."

Simone Lecoutier laughed. "I do not think we can hope to publish it, but we might write out all the recipes for ourselves, and then if any of the others want them, we could lend them our books, and they could copy them."

"We'll publish if we can," said Jo decidedly. "We've got all sorts of continental recipes, and people might like to have them. Righto! Let's start. What shall we begin with?"

"Soups, of course." Simone, the Frenchwoman, sounded as decided as Jo. "Have you paper, Jo? And your pen? Then let us begin."

And that is how the *Chalet Girls' Cook Book* was born. The four chums had been spending a holiday together in a chalet at Buchenhaus; and three days after they had arrived, the young son of their landlady had gone down with mumps. As there were small children in all their homes save Simone's, and as none of them had ever had this distressing ailment, the elders had decreed that they must stay where they were till quarantine was over. And then it started to pour with rain! Hence their boredom; and hence, when Simone, the housewifely, suggested that they should amuse themselves by collecting together their pet recipes to give to Marie, who was betrothed and to be married before long, someone had suggested they should compile a cookery book. Now, they gathered round the centre table, Jo with a sheaf of foolscap before her, pen in hand, and a big bottle of ink at one side; and they forgot the weather and possible mumps as they bent their minds to their task.

"Soups first," said Marie. "Where shall we start?"

"The stockpot!" cried Simone. "You cannot make soup without that. We always have a stockpot at home, and so we always have stock for soup."

"Your job, then," said Jo. "Carry on! How do you begin?"

"With the pot," said her friend promptly. "A large pot, too. Here is what you should put in it."

>THREE LB. OF BONES—SHIN OF BEEF OR VEAL
>THREE QUARTS OF WATER

A LITTLE SALT

A HERB BOUQUET—A SPRIG EACH OF PARSLEY, MARJORAM, THYME, AND BAY LEAF, TIED TOGETHER

Set on the stove, and bring very slowly to the boil. Then you must skim off the fat as it rises, and keep gently boiling for four or five hours. After that, you strain off the liquid. When the stock is quite cold, you must remove any fat remaining."

"It sounds a long job," said Jo, writing hard.

"I know. But stock is the foundation of many soups, and also of gravy and sauces. Now write again, Jo," and she continued: "Do not over-season or over-flavour, for stock is *only* a foundation, and it will depend on what kind of soup you wish to make how it should be flavoured. You may add almost any kind of vegetables to stock for a vegetable soup: carrots, parsnips, turnips, onions, cabbage, leeks. All these are savoury if added to stock. Jo, you know Maman's pot-au-feu made with cabbage. Well, this is the recipe."

"It's ambrosia!" said Jo. "And I also love her potage—"

"That is thick soup. Clear or thin soup is consommé—very good for tiny children."

"But you can use fish also," put in Frieda. "And oh, Jo! You had better add that it is well not to make thick soups *too* thick!"

They all began to giggle. Jo's one attempt at soup in their cookery class had been so thick that it had needed a knife to cut it.

"I think," said Marie, "that we had better leave out consommés beyond just this mention. They are so difficult to get really good."

"Right you are," said Jo cheerfully. "Now, what next?"

"I will give you our favourite soup," said Frieda. And she dictated:

EVERYDAY SOUP

Cut up, very finely, carrots, parsnips, turnips, celery—any or all of these vegetables. Place them in a panful of stock, and cook gently—don't you call it 'simmer'?—then simmer. You may add macaroni, vermicelli, spaghetti, or rice. Serve with a little finely-chopped parsley sprinkled over the top."

"Your turn, Marie," said Jo, as she finished this.

"Very well, then. I will give you our

POTATO SOUP

> FOUR LARGE POTATOES
> ONE ONION
> SALT AND PEPPER

Boil the potatoes, but don't let them get too soft. Then strain off the water, and add to the potatoes 1½ pints of milk—fresh, tinned, or that powdered milk one can buy. Chop your onion very finely, and add that. Then simmer all till the potatoes have gone. Strain through a sieve, and put the soup into a saucepan, and simmer again with just a small piece of butter or margarine. Serve with a sprinkling of chopped parsley."

"We could manage that in Guide camp," said Jo. "Simone, another idea from you, please!"

"What about Maman's cauliflower soup?"

"The very thing! Go ahead!"

So Simone began:

CAULIFLOWER SOUP

Take one large cauliflower, or two or three small ones. Soak it in salt water, and then break up into small pieces, which are put in boiling salted water, and cooked till tender. When it is done, remove it, and pour on the sauce which you make while it is cooking. Here it is:

> ONE TABLESPOONFUL OF MARGARINE OR BUTTER
> TWO TABLESPOONFULS OF FLOUR

Melt the fat in a saucepan, but don't let it brown."

"Why not?" asked Jo, writing briskly.

"Because that would ruin it. Stir in the flour, and add one pint of milk and cauliflower water, mixed. Boil it, and stir with a wire whisk so that you have no lumps. You should mix with a whisk, too. When your cauliflower is soft, drain it, and pour on the sauce. Then put it all through a sieve, and add a pinch of sugar, a sprinkling of grated nutmeg, and, if your soup is too thick—I know you, Jo!—thin it with a little more milk and cauliflower water. Serve very hot. If you want another flavouring, grate a little cheese over it before you serve. And now it is your turn!"

"Right! I'm going to give you a real English soup—Scotch Broth!" said Jo; and was instantly embroiled in an attempt to explain how *Scotch* Broth could possibly be an *English* soup.

"Well, I don't know; but it is!" she cried finally. "I dare say old James I brought it with him from Scotland and we adopted it. Anyway, here it is for you. I'll say it as I write." And she began:

SCOTCH BROTH—ACCENT ON THE 'SCOTCH'!

TWO LB. OF NECK OF MUTTON, AND ANY OTHER MUTTON BONES
TWO GOOD-SIZED CARROTS, TWO DITTO TURNIPS
TWO ONIONS, OR TWO LEEKS
ONE STICK OF CELERY
ONE LARGE CUP OF BARLEY
ONE LARGE CUP OF LENTILS—*soaked overnight, or they won't soften*
PEPPER AND SALT TO TASTE

Put your bones and meat into a pan with two quarts of water; add the barley and lentils, and let them boil with the lid on till nearly cooked. Cut up the vegetables into small cubes, and pop them in with the pepper and salt, and simmer for two hours. By the way, if you let it boil, it comes queer and thin, so *don't*! Sprinkle on a little chopped parsley just before serving. Grand for a cold day!"

"You aren't putting *that* into the recipe?" cried Marie, aghast.

"Why not? That's just a tip not to try it in boiling weather."

"Oh, *you*! Well, now I'm going to give you our Spinach Soup."

And Marie began carefully:

SPINACH SOUP

Wash 2 lb. of spinach, and then put it into one pint of boiling water, and cook quickly *with* the lid on. Strain and put through a sieve. If too thin, thicken the soup with a little milk and water mixed to a cream. Pour back into the saucepan, add a tablespoonful of butter or margarine, a little grated nutmeg, and pepper and salt. Mix well, and reheat. This must be served *very* hot. If you like to do things really well, fry some bread, and cut this into tiny pieces, and stir in, too. Now it's Frieda's turn. What will you give us, Frieda?"

Frieda finished counting the stitches on her stocking heel, and then said, "I think—Tomato Soup."

"All pink and creamy," said Jo greedily. "Carry on!"

TOMATO SOUP

ONE LB. TOMATOES
ONE CARROT
ONE ONION
TWO CLOVES
ONE BOUQUET OF HERBS
ONE TEASPOONFUL OF SUGAR
ONE QUART OF WATER
ONE OZ. OF BUTTER OR MARGARINE
ONE OZ. OF FLOUR
PEPPER AND SALT

Cut up the vegetables, and boil them with the herb bouquet till they are quite soft. Take out the herbs, and rub the remainder through a sieve. Melt the butter, stir in the flour, and add the milk to it, and boil this till it thickens. Then pour it over the sieved vegetables. Boil up again, and add the salt and pepper."

"Any trimmings?" asked Jo.

"If you want to be grand, you can serve boiled rice, vermicelli, or fruit sippets—that's Marie's scraps of bread, only of fruit this time—in it."

"Fruit sounds a bit startling," said Jo, as she finished the recipe. "Still, it might be a nice change. Who's next?"

"You!" Three voices answered her.

"If I do the writing—oh, all right! Here's

PEA SOUP

    SOME BACON OR HAM BONES
    HALF LB. OF SPLIT PEAS, SOAKED OVERNIGHT
    ONE ONION
    ONE STICK OF CELERY
    ONE CARROT
    ONE QUART OF STOCK
    PEPPER AND SALT

Now then! Cut up the vegetables very finely, and add them and the peas to your stock which you have made as Simone said, but from the pig bones."

"*Jo!*" shrieked the others in horror.

"Well, bacon and ham *are* pig, aren't they? Now, let me finish. Cook gently until the peas are soft. Skim off your *scum*, and pass the soup through a sieve and reheat. You won't want much salt, so be careful. Ham and bacon have their own salt, you know. Serve with dried mint, and if you like to be extravagant, sippets of bacon."

"That reminds me," said Simone, "what about Green Peapod Soup?"

"You can't cook peapods. Don't be an ass, Simone."

"Oh, yes, you can. You English are extravagant in your cooking. We make a delicious soup out of them, and I will give you the recipe for our book. Then you can try it some time and see for yourself."

"I doubt if I ever do. But carry on with your recipe." And Jo picked up the pen, and prepared to write once more.

Simone began at once. "Use the young, tender pods. Cover them with water, and add an onion and some fresh mint. Cook till everything is soft. Take out the mint—the best way is to put it into a little muslin bag for the cooking—and pass the rest through a sieve. Return to the saucepan with a little margarine, a pinch of sugar and salt, some milk, and some of the water in which the vegetables have been cooked. Reheat, and serve very hot. Really, Jo, it is delicious."

"I'll wait till I've tried it," quoth the sceptic. "Oh, how my hand aches! I'll do one more, and that will be enough. We've got eight soups now, besides all Simone had to say about making stock, and that's enough. Who's going to be the final victim?"

"Me!" cried Marie. "I'll give you a Russian recipe this time—Bortch! It's very special."

"Very well. But when we've got that down, I think we'll let up for to-day, and have a game of Rummy. Out with it, Marie!"

Marie laughed. "Here you are, then:

BORTCH SOUP

ONE LB. LEAN BEEF CUT UP SMALL
ONE SOUP BONE
THREE CARROTS, CHOPPED INTO DICE
THREE SMALL ONIONS SLICED
THREE STICKS OF CELERY, CHOPPED FINE
TWO QUARTS OF WATER
TWO UNCOOKED BEETROOTS CHOPPED
PEPPER AND SALT
A BOUQUET OF HERBS

"I thought you couldn't chop beetroots uncooked?" said Jo.
"You do for this though. Go on, Jo! Here is the method."
Jo took up her pen again with a groan, and wrote:
"Put the beef, bone, carrots, celery, onions, and water into a saucepan, and bring *slowly* to the boil. Put in your herb bouquet, and cook for two hours—just simmering. Strain, and season to taste. Then add your chopped beets, and simmer again for fifteen minutes. Serve"—Marie's eyes grew mischievous—"serve with a dollop of sour cream whipped up as stiff as you can."
"I don't believe you," said Jo flatly.

"But it is so. And lots of people eat the meat and vegetables after. It's a lovely soup, Jo, but don't forget you must never *boil* it—just simmer."

"I'd better make a special note for all those young people who think that when you make soup you've got to *boil* it!" Jo wrote down the last ingredient, added a large, "Never *boil* soup—only *simmer*," at the bottom, and then laid down her pen finally, and rubbed her wrist with a sigh of relief. "That's enough for to-day. Frieda, get the cards, there's a lamb!"

FISH

FISH

THE next three days were fine, and the girls were able to be out most of the time. But on the fourth day they awoke to find the clouds down, the rain streaming, and a miserable wind whimpering round the chalet.

"How horrid!" said Marie, surveying the outlook mournfully.

"Don't be silly," said Frieda. "Oh, the weather is not nice, I know, but think how much we can do at our cookery book! Let us begin as soon as Mittagessen is over; and write letters this morning, and darn our stockings."

"You *would* think of stockings!" said Jo, with a groan. "However, short of going about barelegged, I shall have to do something about mine, so I suppose we'd better."

Accordingly, after a busy morning, they sat round the table when Mittagessen (or lunch) was over. Frieda and Simone had their embroidery; but Marie refused to do anything, and Jo was armed with her pen, since once more she was to be the scribe.

"What now?" she asked. "Fish, I suppose, since it comes after soup. Who's going to do the opening part? Simone, will you oblige?"

Simone laughed. "Beyond the fact that you must be careful to use only *fresh* fish, I do not see that there is any need for further introduction," she said.

"Yes; but how do you know whether it's fresh or not—short of smelling it?" demanded Jo. "You can't very well go round the fishmonger's *sniffing* at his goods. He might object!"

"*Jo!* What a suggestion!" cried the scandalised Simone. "You look to see that the flesh is firm, the gills bright red, and the eyes full and clear."

"Well," said Jo wickedly, "I've done a few queer things in my time, but I never imagined I should come to gazing fondly into the eyes of a young cod! However, you never know what lies before you! All right; I've got that down. Now, what else? What about kinds of fish? And do stop giggling, you three!"

"Well, there are white fish, such as your cod," said Simone, with a chuckle, "and haddock, hake, whiting, and soles and plaice. They need fat for cooking, as most of theirs is in the liver—"

"I know—cod-liver oil!" agreed Jo, with a shudder.

"And that is always removed for cooking," continued Simone placidly, being accustomed to Jo's remarks.

"I should think so! I've done that. Are there any fish which have natural oil—I mean in their flesh, so to speak?"

"Of course: herring, mackerel and salmon are all oily. They are more nourishing than the white ones, but harder to digest. Such fish should be even fresher than white fish if that is possible. They make valuable food, being full of protein."

"*I'm* not a scientist," quoth Jo, scribbling busily. "Anything else we ought to mention?"

"Oh, Simone! What about shell-fish?" asked Marie.

"They are usually expensive, and generally indigestible. They include lobster, prawns, crab, shrimps, crayfish, and oysters."

"And winkles—which you eat with a pin," added Jo.

"Also mussels," said Simone, giving her interrupter a severe look. "Oysters, when raw, are easily digested. You often give them to invalids for that reason. But do not try that if they are cooked."

"Why not?"

"Because then they are most *in*digestible. Fish," continued Simone, warming to her subject, "can be baked, steamed, fried, and boiled."

"Thanks; I know all about *frying* fish," said Jo, whose efforts in that line had roused the cookery mistress to complete horror.

The rest chuckled at the reminiscence, and Marie said, "If you would wait until your fat is boiling, and then cook carefully, you would soon manage it."

"Never!" retorted the pessimist. "I can manage baked fish, but fried fish is beyond me."

"Well, as your stuffed haddock was simply delicious, I'll grant you can do that," returned Marie, with the air of one conferring a great favour. "Suppose we start off with your recipe."

"I don't mind; so here goes."

"Repeat it aloud as you write, please," said Simone, "in case you forget anything and we can remind you."

"Of all the insults! Oh, all right! Now then:

STUFFED BAKED HADDOCK

Stuffing

TWO OZ. STALE BREAD
TWO TEASPOONFULS CHOPPED PARSLEY
ONE OZ. MELTED MARGARINE
PEPPER AND SALT

Soak the bread in either milk or water; squeeze out the moisture, and then beat thoroughly with a fork. Add the seasonings, and beat again. Add the margarine. This is enough for a 2 lb. haddock, by the way. Make sure your fish is scaled." Jo suddenly stopped writing and began to laugh. "Do you remember when Corney forgot that fish *have* scales and cooked hers with them on? Wasn't there a fuss?"

The rest laughed. Frau Mieders, the Chalet School cookery mistress, had certainly expressed herself to the said Corney with great bitterness, for, as it happened, there had been guests to Mittagessen that day; and the baked haddock was to have been the pièce de résistance.

"Better add, 'be sure that it is cleaned'," said Frieda.

"*And* dried," chimed in Simone.

"It might be as well." Jo wrote hard for a minute or so, and then went on with her recipe.

"Pack the fish with the stuffing, and sew it up with a darning-needle and strong cotton. Have some hot fat in a dripping tin; place the fish on a trivet in the tin, and bake in a moderate oven, basting frequently for twenty minutes—a little longer if the fish is not done. Decorate with parsley and lemon and serve."

"What sauce with it, Jo?" asked Marie.

"Oh, any sauce. But it was awfully good with that cucumber cream you made the same day, Simone. Let's say that."

Jo finished it, and then said, "And now, Simone, we'll come down on you. What do you propose to contribute?"

"Lobster cutlets," said Simone briskly. "Are you ready?"

Jo wrote LOBSTER CUTLETS and waited.

HALF PINT OF BÉCHAMEL SAUCE

began Simone.

"Of *what*?" demanded Jo.

"Béchamel sauce!"

"It is just another name for white sauce."

"Oh, I see. All right. Go on!"

HALF PINT OF BÉCHAMEL SAUCE
ONE TIN LOBSTER OR CRAYFISH—IF YOU CANNOT GET FRESH

A FEW PIECES OF MUSHROOM IF POSSIBLE
EGG AND BREADCRUMBS

I will give the sauce first, Joey, just in case anyone forgets. Melt one tablespoonful of fat, and mix with it a heaped tablespoonful of flour, and cook gently, being careful not to brown. Add slowly half a pint of milk, stirring all the time until the sauce thickens. It should be very thick this time, by the way; if you are using tinned fish, you can use some of the juice instead of all the milk, or if you use all milk, and prefer it, you can flavour with a very little Essence of Anchovies. While the sauce is warm, add your fish, flaked, and the mushrooms—if you have got them. Let the mixture grow quite cold, then shape it into cutlets—you had better draw a cutlet-shape, Jo."

"Anything to oblige." And Jo carefully drew the shape. "That all?" she queried.

"No; they are to be cooked yet. When you have shaped your cutlets, roll them well in flour before you egg and breadcrumb them. Beat your egg to a good froth, and if it is not enough, you may add a very little milk. Dip each cutlet in, and then roll in very fine breadcrumbs. Fry in hot fat to a golden brown, and serve with sprigs of fried parsley."

"Now that's another thing I never get right," said Jo, pausing. "Yours always keep their colour, Simone, but mine come out a muddy brown. What is the why of that?"

"You fry them too long," returned Simone promptly. "They should be in the pan only two seconds at most. And, of course, you should wash the pan well, and see that it is quite dry first."

"Well, I know what this tastes like," said Jo, "but it strikes me as an awful bother to make. I should say this is one of those Very Special Occasion Dishes."

"I will give you a contrast," said quiet Frieda with a smile. "Here is

POACHED KIPPERS

Cut off the heads of the kippers, put them in hot water, and then dry them. Place them in a frying-pan with just enough cold water to cover them, and bring them to the boil. Simmer for one minute longer, then serve on a hot dish, with a dab of butter on each."

"And here is a—a kind of extension of that," put in Simone. "These are

SCRAMBLED KIPPERS

Take a poached kipper, remove the bones, and put it through a sieve. Place in a small saucepan with a tablespoonful of milk, a knob of butter or margarine, one egg, and a sprinkle of pepper. Kippers *are* salt, so do not need any added. Stir until the mixture looks like scrambled eggs, and serve on slices of hot buttered toast. If you prefer a more delicate flavour, you can use smoked haddock in the same way."

"I might manage that myself," said Jo. "But what about this frying of which we've all heard so much? Who's going to do it?"

"Marie," said Simone. "She hasn't given us a thing yet."

"You were all so anxious to have your fingers in the pie, there wasn't room for me," retorted Marie. "I'll certainly give you all the tips I can for frying fish, Joey, though really it ought to be Simone. Her fried fish is a genuine creation; but I want to do my share. After all, this is *my* cookery book in the first instance."

"Quite right; so it is. Well, I'm ready if you are," said Jo, sucking the ink off her forefinger.

"There are," began Marie, "*three* ways of frying fish."

"*Three* ways?" demanded Jo. "*How* are there three? I only know two myself; in batter, or in egg and breadcrumbs. What's the third?"

"Just plain—with neither, that is. But you can't use it for any but the oily fish like mackerel and herring. They, as you may remember," added Marie gently, "have oil in their flesh. The others haven't, so need a little assistance."

"Well, let's have the batter process, shall we?"

"Here you are, then. Rub salt and pepper well into the flesh of the fish when you are sure it is quite dry. Then flour, and dip into a well-beaten egg. Make sure that it is well covered. Then put the fish into a pan of boiling fat, and cook gently till it is golden-brown. And by the way, Joey," added her friend, "do you know *how* to tell when fat is boiling?"

"Yes; I do, so don't try to insult me. The smoke rising from it should be bluish in tint. I do know *that*! Now get on with the egg and breadcrumbs."

"I've one or two more things to say about the batter first. You can eat fish cooked this way either hot or cold. The ideal method is to use oil; but failing that, lard or dripping will do."

"Any kind of oil? Would machine oil do?" inquired Jo sweetly.

"Dummkopf! Of course not! *Vegetable* oil—olive is best."

Jo chuckled as she wrote down the last remarks, and Marie, leaning back in her chair, dictated: "In egg and breadcrumbs. Proceed in the same way as for batter, but after you have dipped the fish in the egg, roll it in breadcrumbs. And here's a tip that may help *you*, Jo. If you sprinkle a little salt on the pan before you melt the fat, the fish won't stick."

"I wish I'd known that sooner," grumbled Jo. "Then I mightn't have had so many rows with Frau Mieders. Well, what about plain frying?"

"Very little. It is difficult to do well, for it means simply greasing the bottom of the pan before you put in the fish, and then you cook very, very slowly, to allow the natural fat in the fish to help with the frying. I don't advise *you* to try it, Joey."

"Don't worry; I shan't. Well, is there anything more before we leave fish?"

"Oh, we must have fish-cakes or a fish pie!" cried Frieda. "And there is kedgeree, too."

"We'll have one kind of fish-cake," said Simone. "I can give you a very good one. But Jo must give us the kedgeree, for she makes it well. Jo, should you not say how to have breadcrumbs always in stock?"

"Well, I do know that, for I've seen Madge do it. Collect all your odd bits and pieces of bread, put them in a baking-tin in the oven when it is hot, and leave them till they are golden-brown. Then crush them—I use the rolling-pin and an old pastry board, myself—or you can employ the potato-beater and an enamel bowl, or sieve them. Keep in a tin with a lid, and add others as they go down. That's all."

"Write it down," said Marie sternly. "*We* may know how to do it, but there are people who don't. Then we can have Simone's fish-cakes and your kedgeree. I think that will be quite enough for fish."

"So do I," said Frieda, as Joey wrote down her own directions for keeping a supply of breadcrumbs on hand. "If this bad weather continues, we must do meat dishes to-morrow."

"I'm ready," announced the secretary, sitting up. "Bring on your fish-cakes, Simone."

"You need three-quarters of a pound of potatoes," began Simone. "Mash them thoroughly. To these add some cold cooked fish, or tinned salmon, after you have removed all the bones, and some finely chopped parsley. Moisten all with béchamel sauce, making it into a stiff dough. Whatever you do, do not let it be wet. Let it stand till quite cold. Then make into shapes—round, sausage shape, or you can cut it into squares. Dip each into flour, and then egg and breadcrumb, and fry golden-brown."

"Right!" said Jo. "Now for my

KEDGEREE

ONE OZ. BUTTER OR MARGARINE
ONE HARD-BOILED EGG CUT INTO SLICES

HALF LB. OF COOKED RICE

HALF LB. OF COLD COOKED FISH OR A TIN OF SALMON

Now for the method. Melt the fat in a pan, and add the rice, the egg, and the fish. Season with salt and pepper. For 'them as likes it' you can add a touch of curry, but it should be only a touch. Curry powder is on the powerful side. When the kedgeree is hot, pile it on a warm dish, and decorate it with sprays of parsley and some of the yolk of the egg, which you should keep for the purpose. You must sieve that, so that it makes a golden powder over the white of the rice. The green and white and gold—and pink, if you use salmon—really makes this a very pretty dish."

"I always find rice such a bother," said Frieda. "Look at my rice pudding three terms ago! It was just a sodden mess. Does anyone know how to avoid that?"

"I know one way—the Indian way," said Jo, whose married brother and sister-in-law had been home from India some time before. "Mollie told me."

"Then let's add it," said Marie. "And I have a Chinese method of cooking it as well; and Corney Flower gave me an American recipe for frying rice."

"We shall add them," said Simone with decision. "And then it should be time for Kaffee und Kuchen. Go on, Jo!"

"Well," said Jo, "you wash the rice in several waters, and have ready a large saucepan containing salted water boiling hard. If you have a lemon handy, put in a squeeze of lemon juice. Throw in your rice, and boil fast for twelve or fifteen minutes. When the grains are soft, drain off the water, and then throw a jug of *cold* water over the rice to separate the grains. Drain it thoroughly, and if you want it hot, hot it up again. Your turn, Marie!"

"The Chinese steam their rice," said Marie, "and the grains separate on their own account. But, of course, you must drain it well when it is cooked. As for the fried rice, you fry it in either butter or bacon fat and serve it with rashers of bacon. I've had it at the Flowers', and it was mouth-watering!"

"I never heard of such a word," declared Jo, penning the last instruction. "I believe you invented it yourself."

"No; Corney did. But the rice is all I said. You just try it for yourself!" said Marie, as the door opened, and their landlady came in with the afternoon meal of coffee, cakes, and little fancy rolls.

MEATS

MEATS

IT poured all the evening. The girls forgot their dignity and the fact that they were grown-up young ladies, newly emancipated from school, and played paper games with such results that Simone was nearly reduced to hysterics, and the rest were weak and tearful with laughter. They went off to bed, and snuggled down under the plumeaux—which were very comforting on such a night as this—still giving vent to occasional giggles. And Jo Bettany, when she came down to Frühstück (breakfast) next morning, declared that she had wakened twice during the night, and chuckled over one beautiful "Consequence".

"You people were all asleep," she informed them. "The only noises besides my own giggles were the wind in the trees, and the rain which was coming down in cartloads. It didn't stop for a single instant. Just look at it now!"

"Never mind! Come to Frühstück," said Frieda soothingly. "We can consider what we shall do while we have it—but *not* paper games again, please, Joey. I still ache with laughing."

"We don't need to discuss what we'll do," said Jo briskly, as she dropped into her seat, while Marie sat down behind the coffee-pot. "We must get on with this cookery book. Do you realise that we've had a fortnight's quarantine already—fifteen days, in fact. Once it's over, we shall part for a while. Simone goes off to Paris to her beloved Sorbonne; Frieda will be in Innsbruck at the Mariahilf; Marie goes to

Salzburg, and will be up to the neck in getting ready for her wedding; and I shall be at the Sonnalpe, helping with the babies. If we mean to do it at all, we simply *must* finish before we go home. Once we part, goodness knows when we'll be all together again like this! Push the butter north by east, please."

Following which the orator fell on her Frühstück as if she had not seen food for a month.

After a little more talk, they decided that Jo's idea was a good one; so once the meal was over and they had made their beds and tidied their rooms, Jo sat down at the centre table in the Saal, the others provided themselves with needlework, and they set to work on the Meats part of their cookery book.

"How many ways are there of cooking meat?" asked Jo, as she uncapped her fountain-pen. "Lots, I should say."

Simone threaded her needle with blue silk, and then replied, "There are. The best ways are grilling, roasting, and stewing; and, of course, frying. We had better begin with grilling."

Jo wrote down GRILLING.

"Grilling is an art," began Simone.

"I dare say! You don't expect me to write *that* down?"

"Oh, no. But I just wanted to explain to you that if you can grill really well, then you've learnt something which will be a treasure to you in housekeeping. It is one of the best ways of cooking meat, and the most nourishing. You can make the most appetising dishes this way. Now I'll begin. Are you ready, Jo?"

"And waiting. Carry on!"

"Be sure that your grill is red hot. Grease the grill plate thoroughly. Never salt the meat before grilling, or you will bring out the juices, and as the idea of grilling is to *seal* them in the meat, you will spoil your work at the beginning. Now I am going to give the method."

"I thought that was part of it?"

"Oh, no; just a few hints. This is it now.

"Brush your meat over with a little melted fat before placing on the grid. Leave it for four or five minutes, and then turn. *Never* use a fork for turning. Slip a broad-bladed knife under it; or the special tongs which one can buy for lifting it. When it is done, both sides should be crisp and brown. Serve on a hot dish with little bits of butter and chopped parsley. I'm going to give you a timetable for the most obvious things," continued Simone, "but remember that it is only a general guide. The length of time depends, of course, on the thickness of the meat, and whether you want it well cooked or rather underdone."

"I don't see why you think it's such an art," said Jo, looking at what she had written. "It seems to me that it's just a case of having everything at fever heat, and not sticking pins into it."

"But it *is* an art," returned Simone. "When you are grilling, you must watch the grill the whole time—*and not go into a dream*! Now take down the times.

> RUMP STEAK—EIGHT TO TEN MINUTES
> LAMB CHOPS—EIGHT TO TEN MINUTES
> KIDNEY (SPLIT OPEN)—EIGHT MINUTES
> BACON RASHER—THREE TO FOUR MINUTES

That is all. But please put down that these are not definite times, and underline it."

"Done it! Now what comes next?"

"ROASTING," suggested Frieda, who was busy with an elaborate teacloth intended for Marie, and who had paused to look for her scissors.

"*That's* easy enough, anyhow. Just put your meat into the tin, add some dripping, shove it into the oven, and leave it till done."

"*Jo!*"

"Of course that isn't all." Simone sounded horrified. Marie chuckled and added, "I rather pity the man you marry, Jo! He'll end up by suffering from the worst form of dyspepsia!"

"He doesn't exist, anyhow, so you can save your pity," quoth Jo cheerfully. "I'm going to be an author—famous, if possible! I shan't have any time for husbands and homes and babies! Authoring is a whole-time job, let me tell you, my love!"

"*What* is? I never heard that word before!" said Frieda.

"I dare say not. I've just coined it. Quite neat, I think."

"Your worst enemy could never accuse you of an over-supply of modesty, Jo," said Marie severely. "And as for not marrying, you just wait and see. You never know what may happen."

"You don't—but I don't think *that* will happen. Well, who's going to give me the details of roasting?"

"Me; I've helped often enough at home," said Marie and began:

"The secret of good roasting is to have your oven *hot* before you put your meat in. We cook by electricity, and wait till it registers 300–400. Leave it for ten minutes, and then turn to low. If it is gas, as

Wanda has, then turn your regulo to 8, and when your meat has been in ten minutes, turn down to 6. But you *must* have a hot oven. Have you written all that? Then begin with the actual cooking. Put a lump of fat or dripping into the tin, place in the oven, and melt. When it is smoking hot, put your meat in, and baste it with the fat. When you have poured the hot fat as quickly as you can all over the meat—and you should use a long-handled spoon in case of splashes—put the tin into the oven, and leave for the ten minutes. Then, as I said, turn down to 6, and cook slowly. Baste about every 40 minutes or so to keep the meat from drying, but do it as quickly as possible."

"Is there a timetable to this one?" asked Jo.

"Yes; mutton, pork, and veal take about 20 minutes to each pound and 20 minutes over. For beef, allow 15 minutes to each pound and 15 minutes over. And, by the way, never stick a knife or anything else into your meat to see if it is done. Go by the timetable, and you will be quite safe."

"I've got that. What about gravy?"

"That's Frieda's job. Her gravy is the best. You know what Frau Mieders said at our last lesson."

"I know what she said about mine!" sighed Jo. "Talk about mumps! You never saw anything lumpier than that gravy!"

Frieda smiled. "I'll give you my recipe, Jo, and if you use that, I don't think you'll have many failures."

"I wouldn't be too sure. However, carry on, and we'll see."

"After you have dished the meat, pour off most of the fat, leaving a good tablespoonful in the baking-tin. To this, add a tablespoonful of flour, and a dash of pepper and salt, and fry on the hot plate till it is a rich brown in colour. You should use your basting spoon to smooth it all the time it is frying. Then add some stock from your stockpot; or if you haven't any, some hot water, and bring to the boil, stirring all the time. That is the real secret of smooth gravy. You *must* stir it so that it cooks evenly."

"It seems a lot of bother," said Jo. "Can't you just use some of those powders they advertise and a little water?"

"Certainly not!" cried Simone, lapsing into French. "What an idea!"

"Besides," added Marie, "if you do that, there is no nourishment in your gravy. I don't know about Madame's babies, but Wanda's little Kurt just loves bread and gravy."

"So do ours, if you come to that. Oh, well, I suppose it's got to be done. Now what about frying? Simone—"

"There is only one way to fry meat successfully," replied Simone. "Just grease your frying-pan, and when it is hot, put your meat in, and when one side is brown, turn it with the tongs or a broad knife, and brown the other. Then cook slowly for about ten minutes."

"That seems simple enough. Now, can't we get to some proper recipes? I'm rather bored with all this technical stuff."

"All right," said Marie, who had taken up her hem-stitching, and was progressing with it. "I'll give you a dish you all like: WIENER SCHNITZEL—straight from Wien."

"In other words, Vienna cutlet," translated Jo.

"Yes; as you're writing this in English, I suppose you'd better add that," agreed Marie. "Here is the recipe:

ONE AND A HALF LB. OF VEAL STEAK, CUT HALF INCH THICK
ONE AND A HALF TEASPOONFULS OF SALT
ONE-THIRD CUP OF FLOUR
ONE EGG, LIGHTLY BEATEN
FINE BREADCRUMBS

Cut the veal into six pieces of the same size, and flatten with a rolling-pin or a potato beater. Mix the flour and salt, and rub each piece thoroughly in it; then dip them in the egg, and roll in breadcrumbs. Fry in hot, deep fat until golden-brown; drain, and serve with slices of lemon."

"And served as you do, with cold potato salad, it is just luscious!" supplemented Jo. "Now it's my turn. I haven't given you a single contribution yet. Bianca Meracini gave me her mother's recipe for roast lamb last term, and I remember it, so I'm going to put that in now."

"I hope you *do* remember it!" said Simone gloomily. "I haven't forgotten the time you tried to make Yorkshire tea-cakes from memory, and put in mace instead of mixed spice."

"It wasn't uneatable, anyhow!" retorted Jo. "I admit the flavour was a little—er—unusual; but they weren't too bad."

"Anyhow," put in Frieda, "they weren't anything like as awful as those saffron buns that Joyce Linton *would* make, and she savoured them with sulphur. Do you remember?"

"Do I not?" chuckled Jo. "Corney thought Satan himself had honoured us with a visit!"

"And Bill simply raked everything out of the ovens regardless," Marie chimed in between her peals of laughter. "All those cakes were flat failures, and we had no cake for Kaffee und Kuchen that day!"

The girls shrieked with laughter at the memory. Then they calmed down, and Jo began to write.

ROMAN ROAST LAMB

Use young lamb, so that the meat is really tender. Buy a shoulder, or leg, or loin. Rub it over with a clove of garlic, and salt and pepper. Or, if you like, attach the garlic to the bone. Lay the meat on the rack from the grill, and put in a moderate oven. Baste every twenty minutes with the fat dripping. Serve with a sauce made of red-currant jelly mixed with the juice of an orange.

"That," she added, as she ruled a line beneath the recipe, "is all of that. Now what comes next?"

"I vote Simone gives us a recipe for roast chicken," said Frieda. "Do, Simone. Yours is always so good."

"Very well, if you will give us your mother's recipe for roast goose," agreed Simone. "I never tasted anything better than the one we had that day we were in Innsbruck during the Easter term."

"Oh, you may have that with pleasure. And then, I think we had better go on to stewing meat," said Frieda.

"All right," said Jo. "I'm agreeable. Marie won't want to keep Eugen on roasts all the time."

"Certainly not," said Marie with emphasis, while the pink deepened in her cheeks. "I have a delightful Goulash for you from Hungary."

"It sounds well," said Jo. "Come on, Simone! Let's have your chicken. And before we have the roast goose, I vote we have our 'elevenses'. I'm getting hungry."

"I'll go and ask about it while Simone gives you her recipe," said Marie, getting up. "Hurry up, Simone, and be ready when I come back."

"I don't see those table napkins getting finished this side of the wedding," said Jo, picking up Marie's work. "She's done only—how many? Three, isn't it? And there are a dozen to do in this pattern. Oh, well, it's her affair. Come on, Simone; I'm waiting!"

ROAST CHICKEN

"You need a chicken of three to four pounds in weight," began Simone. "Wash it thoroughly, and truss it after you have rubbed the inside with rough salt. On the outside, rub in fresh lard, salt, and pepper. Place it in a casserole with some butter, and three tablespoonfuls of salted water. Put on the lid, and bake in the oven for about an hour, basting frequently. About ten minutes before serving, remove the lid, and allow the outside skin to brown and crisp. Garnish with sprigs of cress and thin slices of lemon."

"How," asked Jo, as she finished this, "can you tell whether a chicken is a roaster or a boiler? I shouldn't have any idea."

"You roast young birds; old ones must be boiled as they are tough," said Simone.

"Yes; but how do you tell the age?"

"Press the breast-bone. If the bird is young, it will be tender and give. If it doesn't, you may be sure the bird is old. And another way is to look at the legs. Young birds have smooth legs and short spurs. The older a bird, the more scaly the legs look, and the longer the spurs. Also, fowls with black or yellow legs are best for roasting."

"Well," said Jo, "I've got to look into the eyes of a fish to know if it's fresh. Now you tell me to press the breast-bone of a chicken to know if it's young. I'd no idea—" She paused with a wicked look.

"Yes; I think you had *better* be quiet," said Simone with decision. "Really, Jo, one never knows what you will say next!"

"Oh, I was only going to say that it seems to me that fishmongers and poulterers must have a lot to put up with when it comes to customers handling their goods. Here's Marie with 'elevenses'! Chocolate and twists! Good! I feel in need of a little nourishment. All this writing and talking about food gives me an appetite."

As the others felt the same, they put aside their work at once, and settled down to enjoyment of the cups of hot chocolate and twists of fancy bread that Marie had brought. But when they had finished, and the tray had been taken away, Frieda said solemnly, "ROAST GOOSE!"

"Eh?" said Jo, startled, for they had been talking of other things.

"Roast Goose, I said," replied Frieda placidly. "Here is your pen, Joey. I've just refilled it for you. So begin, Liebchen."

"What a lot of slave-drivers you are!" Jo heaved a resigned sigh. "All right; bring on your bears!"

"Die Mutter uses a very old recipe from München—Munich you had better put, I think—which my grandmother gave her. Here it is. Rub the inside of your goose with salt and ground ginger. Stuff with chopped onion, slices of raw potato, and apple, and stitch the skin. Rub the outside with oil or fat, and sprinkle with salt or pepper. Place a grid-iron in your baking-tin, and put the goose on it, and bake in a moderate oven. You should allow twenty minutes' baking to each pound of goose; baste frequently with the fat drippings in the pan. When ready, make a gravy with the fat drippings and stock made from the giblets. Serve with red-currant jelly."

"Then that finishes the roasts," said Jo, stretching. "We'll have your Goulash next, Marie. It sounds most exotic."

"It is no such thing; but a very good savoury dish!" cried Marie indignantly. "You will see!" And she dictated:

HUNGARIAN GOULASH

ONE POUND OF LEAN BEEF CUT INTO SMALL PIECES
ONE POUND OF LEAN VEAL CUT INTO SMALL PIECES
THREE TABLESPOONFULS OF FAT
ONE LARGE ONION CHOPPED FINELY
SALT
ONE TEASPOONFUL OF PAPRIKA PEPPER
ONE CUP OF STRAINED TOMATOES OR TOMATO PURÉE
EIGHT SMALL POTATOES

Melt the fat in a pan and fry the onions and meat till a warm brown. Put them into a casserole with the salt and tomatoes, and cook in a moderate oven for about an hour. Then add the potatoes and paprika, and cook until the potatoes are soft. You can add more potatoes if it is necessary. Serve *very* hot. It is a good dish for a cold day."

"Your turn now, my Jo," said Simone. "What will you give us?"

"I've a good mind to give you nothing after all your remarks about my tea-cakes. But I'll relent and let you have Madge's Lancashire Hot Pot, which really is delicious, and just as good as Marie's Goulash for a cold day." And Jo solemnly inscribed:

LANCASHIRE HOT POT

Fill a large piedish—or you can use a casserole as we do—with layers of potatoes, onions, and neck of mutton chops. Put in a layer of potatoes first, in slices about ¾ inch thick, then a layer of mutton, and after that a layer of onions. Sprinkle each layer with pepper and salt, and go on until your dish is full, finishing off with a double layer of potatoes. By the way, before you put this on," said Jo, ceasing to write, "you should add a little water—not more than will fill say a third of the dish. Put on the last layer, and cover with a tight lid. Place in a slow oven, and bake for 3 or 4 hours—it all depends on how large your Hot Pot is. Most of the water should be used up, leaving the meat moist and tender. This is Lancashire Hot Pot. But you can use the recipe with any other kind of meat, including even corned beef or bacon. It's a useful sort of dish to know."

"It sounds it," said Marie. "Well, is that all?"

Frieda looked up and laughed. "I wonder if you would like Chop Suey?" she said. "Corney gave the recipe one day, and said it was delicious."

"Oh, have it by all means," agreed Jo. "We may as well get as many countries' ideas on cooking into this as we can. Go on, Frieda." And she wrote in her most elaborate script:

CHOP SUEY—CHINESE

ONE LB. OF LEAN PORK

TWO TABLESPOONFULS OF FAT

ONE CUP OF DICED CELERY

TWO CUPFULS OF SLICED ONIONS

ONE CUP OF STOCK—CHICKEN STOCK IF POSSIBLE

THREE-QUARTER LB. OF MUSHROOMS

THREE CUPFULS OF BOILED RICE

SOY SAUCE

Cut up the meat and brown in hot fat. Add the celery, onions, and stock. Cover this, and simmer for 20 minutes. Add one tablespoonful of flour mixed to a smooth paste with water, and stir until the gravy thickens. The Chinese add bean sprouts and Soy sauce."

"What is Soy sauce?" asked Simone curiously.

"It is just Béchamel sauce, only made with soya bean flour instead of with ordinary flour," explained Frieda. "Corney said that their Chinese cook-boy used it frequently. She also said that he generally added a tablespoonful of peanut butter, which gives it a most delicious flavour."

"How long do you cook this mixture?" demanded Jo.

"Until the meat and potatoes are done."

"Does that finish the Meat part of our book?" asked Simone.

"No!" said Jo, with sudden decision. "You ought to have at least one curry, so I'll give you the one my sister-in-law gave Madge just before we came away. We had it for dinner one night, and it was—" Words failed her. She rolled her eyes, and smacked her lips, and the rest burst into peals of laughter.

"You need only to rub your tummy, Jo, and you'd be a perfect picture of greediness personified!" cried Marie.

Jo chuckled. "I don't think I'm greedy; but this really is, as Rix says, 'a bit extra'. I'll put it down, and you can all try it.

MADRAS CURRY

ONE LB. OF ANY KIND OF MEAT—FRESH
ONE LARGE ONION
ONE CLOVE OF GARLIC

TWO OZ. FLOUR

ONE OZ. CURRY POWDER

SALT

Cut up the meat into small pieces, and fry it with the onion and a crushed clove of garlic. If people don't like garlic, you can leave it out. Fry a warm brown. Put into a casserole, and stir in a mixture made of the flour, curry powder, and salt. Add one pint of stock. Cover, and bake in a slow oven until the meat is tender. All sorts of fruit or vegetables may be added to curry, such as raisins, bananas—incidentally, if your curry is too hot, slices of banana will cool it down a little, so to speak—chopped apple, grated coco-nut, sliced green tomatoes. In India, it is served with little pyramids of boiled rice and mango chutney."

"What exactly *is* curry?" asked Marie.

"It's a mixture of all sorts of spices—Indian ones," said Jo readily. "They add turmeric, which gives it its queer colour."

"Well, is *that* all? I should like to mention that it is almost time we cleared the table for Mittagessen," said Simone.

"I think so," Jo was beginning. Then she stopped. "Oh, no! We must have one of our famous Shepherd's Pies! Here's one we sometimes have at the Sonnalpe, and it's quite interesting.

SHEPHERD'S PIE

Put through the mincer any scraps of cold meat, some onions, a few raisins or dates—stone *them* first, or you may regret it!"

"Why?" asked Marie.

"Because you may put your mincer out of action if you try to mince date-stones with it, of course. Now, where was I? Oh yes; here we are. Fill a piedish with this mixture, and season with pepper, salt, and a pinch of mace. Add some strips of bacon, and moisten everything with gravy and tomato purée. Remember, it must neither be too moist nor too dry. Beat some cold mashed potatoes with a little milk until they are creamy, and put a thick layer over everything. Ridge them up with a fork. Then *we* add dabs of dripping here and there, but if you don't like it, you can leave it alone. Put into a hot oven, and bake till the potato is a golden brown, but be careful not to over-cook it. That's the last!"

"Not quite," said Frieda suddenly. "I've just remembered how die Mutter makes her pork-crackling crisp. She rubs the skin with oil and salt before cooking."

"I'll put it in," agreed Jo. "We sprinkle coarse sugar on it, and it improves the flavour of the pork, so I'll put both. There! That really is the last of this section. I can hear Mittagessen arriving, and we must clear. Afterwards, we can give a few recipes for cooking vegetables; and *then*," triumphantly, "we can go on to puddings and cakes!"

VEGETABLES

VEGETABLES

"WELL, now for vegetables!" said Marie as, Mittagessen over, and everything cleared away, they once more settled down.

"Really," grumbled Jo, "it might be November instead of the end of August! What a day!"

"It's nice of Frau Annich to have lighted the stove," said Frieda. "It looks cheerful; and I felt so cold before, even in my woolly."

"We'll write our vegetable recipes," said Jo decidedly. "Then, this evening—"

"No more paper games!" Marie warned her.

"I wasn't going to suggest it. What I *was* going to suggest was that we bring down the little spirit stove and its pan, and ask Frau Annich for some things and make sweets to-night. I could just do with a little fudge or butterscotch!"

"That's a good idea," said Marie approvingly. "We'd better ask her if she can let us have the things before we begin our writing. If not, perhaps someone could go and get them for us."

"That man that does all her odd jobs would go," agreed Jo. "He's not quite all there; but he can do messages. You scoot, Marie. You're her blue-eyed pet. She thinks it's *so* romantic that you're going to be married so soon, and Frau Annich is a romantic soul."

Poor Marie blushed crimson. "Jo, you *are* the limit!" she cried. "Just you see what I'll do when it's your turn! I'll get my own back then!"

"If you wait for that, you'll have a very long time to go, my dear," returned Jo, being no prophetess. "Never mind that. You run along and see if you can't get a few ingredients for sweetstuff out of her. We'll wait till you come back."

Marie cast a glance nicely compounded of impotent fury and despair at Jo, and then went meekly to do as she was asked. She came back to say that they could have what they wanted, and Frau Annich offered to lend them any cooking utensils they needed into the bargain. The other three cheered on hearing this, and then Simone suddenly produced a box of chocolates from her knitting-bag, and handed them round.

"Cheers for Simone, too!" cried the irrepressible Jo, as she bit into a truffle; and they were given with much goodwill. "Now we'll begin," continued the scribe of the party. "Any special comments to make before we get down to recipes, Simone?"

"I don't think so," said her friend consideringly.

"Then how shall we begin?"

"Well, what is the commonest vegetable of all? The potato, of course. We'll begin with it."

Jo rapped on the table with the end of her pen. "Attention, everyone! We will have one way of cooking potatoes from each of us. Frieda, you begin, please."

"Very well, then. I shall begin with NEW POTATOES, and say that they are the easiest of all to cook. Scrape your potatoes—never peel!—put them into boiling, salted water, and boil until soft—but not mushy. Strain the water off into a dish—it can be used to make gravy—and put the potatoes back into the pan with some butter or margarine, and cook for about one minute. Dish, and pour any surplus melted butter over them. Have ready a spoonful of very finely chopped parsley, and dust this on the top. Serve."

"I will take CHIPS for mine," said Simone. "You should remember that the best chips are made with waxy potatoes. Peel them, and cut them into strips about half an inch thickness, and two or three inches long. Soak them in water for about ten minutes, and then dry well in a cloth. Have ready your deep frying pan with the fat at boiling-point. Oil—olive oil—is the best for this, but you can use lard. Use dripping only if you cannot get either of the others. Put your chips into the frying basket if you have one; if not, just put them, carefully, so as not to splash, into the boiling fat. When they rise to the surface, they are cooked. Take them out, and serve in a very hot dish. Chips are things that must be served as hot as possible. By the way, only half-fill your basket. It is quicker in the end, for the chips fry faster, and more evenly. Also, if you have too many in, you may send your fat over the edge and either scald yourself or begin a small fire on the stove."

"Good! I've got all that. Now, Marie; what about you?"

"I shall give ROAST POTATOES," said Marie, who was inordinately fond of them. "Wash your potatoes thoroughly, choosing those of as nearly equal size as possible. Small ones are best, of course. If you cannot get them, then cut the larger ones into two or three pieces. Soak in cold salted water for ten minutes; then drain, and dry thoroughly in a cloth, and put in very hot fat round the meat. Roast for forty-five minutes or so."

"You've left me MASHED POTATOES—and it's the most uninteresting of the lot," said Jo, when she had got Marie's choice down. "Here's the best I can do. Steam some floury potatoes; drain off any water, and put them in the saucepan and set to dry for a minute or two. Mash thoroughly with salt and pepper. Then add a little *hot* milk—never use cold, whatever you do—and a nut of butter or margarine. Beat this thoroughly with a spoon until the whole is light and creamy, then dish, and sprinkle with chopped parsley. By the way, we sometimes put them under the grill for three or four minutes, until they have a delicate, golden top, and then sprinkle the parsley."

"I think that sounds delicious," said Marie with conviction.

"So do I," said Simone. "Well, now I am going to give you a Breton recipe I got from Jeanne le Cadoulec the term before last. They really are delicious things. Are you ready, Jo? Then write:

PUFF-TALLOONS

Mash a pound of floury potatoes, which must be dry. When the potatoes are cool, mix in the yolks of two eggs, salt and pepper. Whisk up the whites of your eggs very stiff until they come up like foam; so that you can turn your plate upside down and they won't fall off—if you do it quickly enough. While you are doing this, have your deep-fat pan coming to the boil. Now beat the whites into the potatoes, and when the fat has stopped bubbling, put in spoonfuls of potatoes, and cook a golden colour. Take out very carefully, and pile on a dish. Garnish with chopped parsley, and serve very hot."

"That sounds golloptious!" said Jo, falling back on a word forbidden in her early schooldays. "I shall try that as soon as I get back to the Sonnalpe."

"Try this, too," said Frieda eagerly. "It is a luncheon dish, or you could use it for Abendessen. I will give you quantities for four people, and I am sure you will like it." And she dictated:

POTATO CREAMS

FOUR LARGE POTATOES
TWO OZ. OF GRATED CHEESE
HOT MILK
PEPPER AND SALT

Wash the potatoes, and make a slit in the side of each. Bake them in their skins—don't you say 'jackets', Jo?—until soft; about an hour should be long enough. Cut round the slits, and remove the insides. Those you put into a basin and mash. Add your cheese, seasoning, and hot milk, and beat till it is like thick cream. Fill the potato cases with this, and grate some more cheese over them. Then bake under the grill."

Jo finished writing this down. Then she looked solemnly round on her friends. "I thought you all loved me," she said plaintively.

"What on earth do you mean?" demanded Marie, wide-eyed.

"Well," said wicked Jo, "I once read a magazine article which said that if you ate too many potatoes, the diet caused your upper lip to grow long. I'm sure that I should look like the chief wonder at a freak show if I had a very long upper lip, and yet here are all you people giving me such savoury recipes that I *must* make them or burst; and I'm sure I shall make a real pig of myself over them. I call it most incon—" She got no farther, for Marie picked up a cushion lying at hand and launched it at her, and the next few minutes were a hurly-burly from which the chief provocatrice emerged very much tousled, but evidently greatly refreshed, for she picked up her pen again, and demanded, "Well; what next?"

"Didn't we mention Marie's Cucumber Cream when we were doing fish?" asked Frieda. "What about having that, Jo?"

"Good idea! Stop fiddling with your hair, Marie, and begin. I'm ready."

"It's more than I am," was the rueful reply. "*You* may not mind looking like a gollywog gone mad; but *I* don't want anyone to see me with my hair all over like this."

Jo ran her fingers through her black locks, which were in process of growing, and had not quite reached her shoulders. "I suppose I'd better see if I can find a few hairpins. I forgot my hair was no longer bobbed." There was a brief interval while hair-dressing was the order of the day. Then they sat down again, and Marie dictated:

CUCUMBER CREAM

Take a fat ridge cucumber—two, if it is meant as a separate dish for more than two people. Peel them, and cut into rounds an inch thick. Place these in a basin with some salt and vinegar, and let them stand for an hour. Then drain off the vinegar, and put the cucumber into a saucepan with 2 oz. of butter or margarine, a little grated nutmeg, and a teaspoonful of castor sugar, and cook very slowly with the saucepan-lid on until they are soft—this takes about half an hour. Make a white sauce—Béchamel foundation, but add salt. Pour the liquid off the cucumbers, and put them into a greased baking dish or casserole. Cover them with the white sauce, and brown under the grill."

"And very nice, too," said Jo cheerfully. "Well, what next? Simone, you come from the country that can do marvels with cabbage and spinach. Can't you give us some tips? You know how most people dislike either."

Simone laughed. "For cooking CABBAGE, I think the best way is to cut the cabbage across into shreds—very fine ones. Place in a saucepan with a very little boiling salted water, and put the lid on. Cook for about ten minutes. You can cook brussels sprouts and curly kale in the same way. For SPINACH, it is a little different."

"How?" demanded Jo.

"Well, to begin with, you should add practically *no* water to spinach. Wash it well in salted water, and put it into a saucepan. If you like you may put two teaspoonfuls of the water with it, but if you are a really good cook, you won't need even that. Cook for ten minutes, shaking the pan frequently to prevent the spinach from burning. Turn out into a hair sieve and drain. It should come out looking like green velvet if it is properly done."

"Your turn, Jo," said Frieda.

"I don't know what to give you. I think I'll tell you how we cook PEAS. Put them into a saucepan of boiling water with a teaspoonful of sugar and a pinch of salt. Add a sprig or two of mint, and boil steadily but *not* quickly. And don't overboil, or they come out a green mush. When they are done, drain them after you have taken out the mint, and put them into a hot vegetable dish. If you want to be extravagant, put a dab of butter on top."

"And now, I will give you our way of cooking them," said Simone. "Take this down, Joey, and be careful with the ingredients.

PEAS: FRENCH METHOD

ONE CUP OF TEPID WATER
NUT OF BUTTER OR MARGARINE
A FEW SHALLOTS
THE HEART OF A LETTUCE
PEAS
A LITTLE SUGAR AND SALT

Put the peas into the tepid water with the sugar and salt, and pour into your pan—a double-boiler is the best for this, by the way. Add your fat, shallots, and lettuce heart. Put on the lid tightly, and cook until soft but not broken. Drain, and serve with the lettuce."

"A rather more elaborate business than mine," said Jo blandly. "However, I dare say it's quite pleasant when done. Frieda, what about you? What are *you* going to give us?"

"My parsnip pie. You know, Joey, I cannot understand why so many of you English girls dislike parsnips so much. If you would try this, I am sure you would never dislike them again."

"I doubt it," said Jo sceptically. "I don't know about other people, but I'm sure I was born hating parsnips. But carry on."

Frieda laughed, and gave the recipe.

PARSNIP PIE

Cook one pound of parsnips in salted water until soft. Drain and mash them. Add a small piece of butter and some hot milk. Beat until creamy. Put in a greased, fireproof dish, and brown under the grill."

"H'm! I dare say it *might* make them edible," said Jo critically, as she finished penning this. "I don't say I'll try it; but I'll pass the recipe on to Madge. If she likes to make it, I'll sample a little." This with the air of one conferring a great favour.

Frieda only chuckled. Jo could rarely ruffle her placidity, though Marie frequently "rose"; and Simone could be indignant at times, even with her adored Jo, when that young woman had set out to be really annoying.

"Let us do tomatoes now," said Marie. "I have a lovely recipe."

"Oh, so have I!" cried Simone. "It really is delicious."

"I've got one, too," laughed Frieda. "Jo, what about you?"

"Oh, I've *got* one. I don't say it's very elaborate, but it makes quite a pleasing breakfast or supper dish. Right you are! We'll go on to tomatoes. Who's going first? Simone, what about you?"

Simone nodded. "Mine is

AVIGNON TOMATOES

AS MANY TOMATOES AS YOU REQUIRE
OLIVE OIL—PROVENÇAL IF YOU CAN GET IT
A LITTLE FINELY CHOPPED GARLIC
A PINCH OF SUGAR
SOME ROUNDS OF TOAST

If you want this dish to be really successful, you must use Provençal oil; but if you can't get that, any good olive oil will do. Put a little into a frying-pan, and add a little very finely chopped garlic. It must be just a pinch or two. Remember that garlic is very—"

"Pungent," Jo finished for her. "We know all about that. Remember the time Corney flavoured her apple pie with garlic cloves?"

They all shrieked with laughter at the memory. At length they sobered down, and Jo consented to continue with the writing.

"When the oil is hot, put in the tomatoes cut into halves, some pepper and salt, and a pinch of sugar. Fry very slowly till brown. Have ready some rounds of toast, and place two half tomatoes on each. Sprinkle with finely chopped parsley, and serve."

"It should be delicious," said Marie. "What is yours, Frieda?"
"I call it

LOTUS FLOWER TOMATOES

FOUR LARGE TOMATOES
FOUR TABLESPOONFULS OF COOKED CHICKEN OR VEAL
TWO TABLESPOONFULS OF COOKED HAM OR TONGUE
ONE TABLESPOONFUL OF FINELY-CHOPPED PARSLEY
SOME SALAD CREAM OR MAYONNAISE
PEPPER AND SALT
LETTUCE LEAVES

Cut the tomatoes in halves, and take out some, but not all, of the pulp. Mince up the chicken and ham or whatever meat you have, and add the parsley. Moisten this with salad cream, and fill the tomatoes with the mixture. Serve on crisp lettuce leaves."

Jo finished writing this down, and looked at it with a frown. "You know," she said slowly, "some of these recipes strike me as rather extravagant in their ingredients. I mean, supposing some of the poorer girls bought the book—if it's ever published—how are they going to get chicken and ham and tongue? Could you use any other kind of meat with it, Frieda?"

"Oh, yes," said Frieda readily. "Almost any kind of meat would do. The recipe says chicken and ham, but there's no need to keep to that."

"Good! Then I'll just add a footnote to say that it is so." And Jo's face cleared as she scribbled her footnote.

"Now it's my turn," said Marie. "Mine is called:

VENETIAN LADIES

FOUR LARGE TOMATOES
TWO CUPS OF FRESHLY-COOKED GREEN PEAS OR FRENCH BEANS
ONE FINELY CHOPPED SHALLOT
ONE FINELY CHOPPED RASHER OF HAM OR BACON
SUGAR, SALT, PEPPER, AND A PINCH OF MINCED MINT
GRATED CHEESE—PARMESAN, FOR CHOICE

Cut the tomatoes in half, and scoop out the pulp. Fill the tomato case with the peas or beans, shallot, rasher, and seasoning which you will have previously mixed together. Put them into a buttered baking dish, and cover thickly with grated cheese. Bake for ten minutes. Serve on slices of fried bread cut into rounds."

"Isn't it rather finicky to make?" asked Jo.

"Well, it is; but it does if you want a special dish for Mittagessen or Abendessen when visitors come.

By the way, the Venetians sometimes use chopped garlic instead of shallots, and also add a sprig of fennel."

"Apart from Ophelia—or was it Perdita?—I don't believe I've ever met fennel in anything," said Jo. "What's it like?"

"Oh, very pretty, and it tastes of aniseed."

"Well, it would be a most decorative affair, I should imagine. My poor effort is very homespun after this! But it's jolly good for all that, and I am not ashamed of it, so here goes:

TOMATO SCRAMBLED EGGS

> TWO EGGS
> ONE OZ. OF BUTTER OR MARGARINE
> THREE TABLESPOONFULS OF TOMATO PULP
> PEPPER AND SALT
> A PINCH OR TWO OF SUGAR

Beat the eggs well, and add pepper and salt, pulp, and sugar. Melt the butter in a saucepan, and then add eggs and tomatoes. Stir until set, but do not let boil. Serve in mounds on rounds of hot buttered toast."

"Jo! That's just scrambled eggs with a change of flavouring!" cried Marie. "You won't get off with just that, so don't think it! Produce another recipe, and produce it quickly!"

"Don't know another!"

"I'm sure you do! We had a whole list of tomato recipes from Frau Mieders last term, and she told us each to find one for ourselves and write it out for her. What was yours?"

Jo screwed up her face in an effort to remember, while the rest watched her with interest.

Finally: "If you go on making faces like that, your face will turn inside out," said Frieda unexpectedly. "It cannot need so many grimaces to remember, Jo!"

"I've got it," said Jo, relaxing her efforts and her face at the same time, rather to the relief of the others, who had begun to fear she would strain some muscle if she went on. "Mine was

BAKED STUFFED TOMATOES

FOUR LARGE TOMATOES
ONE EGG
ONE OZ. GRATED CHEESE
TWO TABLESPOONFULS BREADCRUMBS
PEPPER AND SALT
NUT OF BUTTER OR MARGARINE

Cut off the tops of the tomatoes, hollow out centre, and turn upside down to drain. Whip up your egg, and add the grated cheese, breadcrumbs, and the butter in tiny dabs. Fill the tomatoes with this, and replace the tops as lids. Put into a greased baking dish, and cover with greased paper. Bake in a moderate oven for ten minutes. Dish up each tomato on a round of toast, and add a spray of parsley by way of ornamentation."

"That's quite as pretty as any of ours," said Frieda. "But oh, Jo! Do stop making faces like that! You'll hurt yourself if you do it so—so violently! I felt quite alarmed."

Jo chuckled. "No need to worry, my child. My face is made of best india-rubber. You watch!" And she produced a grimace so fearful as to outdo altogether any she had previously managed.

"Jo! Stop it!" cried Marie, as well as she could in the midst of the laughter. "It's getting late, and we haven't said a thing about mushrooms yet. And Simone has a mixed vegetable dish, I know. Do stop making yourself uglier than you need be, and get on with the writing!"

Jo promptly looked as solemn as a judge, and picked up her pen again. "I'll take down two recipes for mushrooms, but no more. I never knew anything like it," she went on plaintively. "The more you people produce, the more you seem to *want* to produce. We'll have Simone's mixed affair after the mushrooms, and then I'm going to strike. I've done enough for one day. I shall be getting writer's cramp at this rate."

Warned by her tone, Frieda hurriedly dictated:

MUSHROOMS ON TOAST

Toast as many rounds of bread as you require, butter on *both* sides—"

"What sinful extravagance!" cried Jo.

"It isn't! It is part of the recipe. Do go on, Joey! Butter on both sides, and place the rounds in a fireproof baking dish. Peel your mushrooms and place them head downwards on the pieces of toast. Sprinkle them with a little salt and pepper, and place a small piece of butter or margarine on each round. Cover with a lid, and bake in the oven for fifteen minutes. Serve with grilled rashers of bacon. By the way, save your mushroom peelings and stalks, for they can be used for flavouring soups and stews."

"Talking of flavouring," said Simone, passing her chocolates again, "Irma told me that in Russia they gather mushrooms, and thread them on thick white double cotton, and then hang them up to dry so that they can have them for use at any time. You don't peel the mushrooms. You just wipe them, cut off their stalks, and string them like beads. When you have a long enough chain, you hang them up in gentle warmth till they are dry. They shrivel up till they look like little beads. Irma said they will keep for months like this. When you want them, you just soak them in water, and they swell almost to their natural size."

"I say! That's a useful tip!" exclaimed Jo. "Well, there's our two mushroom recipes. And I've just remembered an Australian pumpkin one we might put in. It's made from the Australian pumpkin they call 'Ironback', because the rind is so hard. You peel the pumpkin, cut it into fairly large pieces, which you roll in flour, and bake round the joint like potatoes. It's called Turk's Cap."

"But we do not live in Australia. Could you use any other kind?" asked Simone.

"I expect so. Anyhow, you could try."

"Yes; I will. And now for our last vegetable dish, I am going to give you

VEGETABLE SURPRISE

ONE LB. OF SMALL NEW POTATOES
ONE LB. OF CARROTS
TWO LB. OF PEAS
ONE LETTUCE HEART
ONE RASHER OF BACON
A NUT OF MARGARINE
TWO SMALL SHALLOTS
A LITTLE BOILING WATER
PEPPER AND SALT
ONE TEASPOONFUL OF SUGAR

Put the fat into a saucepan and melt it, but do not brown it, whatever you do. Add the potatoes, nicely scraped, and dried in a cloth; the carrots cut up into rounds, and the shallots finely chopped. Cook these slowly until the potatoes are golden. Don't let it burn, though, or the whole thing will be ruined. Then put in the rasher, cut into small pieces, the peas, salt and pepper, sugar, and half a cup of boiling water. Lastly add the lettuce heart. Put the lid on tightly, and cook slowly until the vegetables are soft. You can serve it with or without grilled bacon, just as you like."

"Well, I think it's a nice climax to this section, so we'll call it a day," said Jo.

CREAMS AND PUDDINGS

CREAMS AND PUDDINGS

"**P**UDDINGS," said Marie, as she threaded a needle, "can be most delightful. One can make them so pretty."

"When you've a crowd of small people, as we have, you concentrate more on making them *filling*," said Jo, who was filling her pen.

"Then we must have recipes for both," decreed Frieda. "What shall we begin with?"

"Never end your sentences with a preposition," was Jo's didactic comment on this. "As for what we shall begin with, I suppose it'll be pastry. Simone—Marie; both of you came out top for pastry, so you can do it between you. I'm ready now, so let's start."

"Very well," said Simone. "And first, I want to say that the most important thing to remember in making pastry is to handle it as little as possible once you have mixed your dough; and to remember also to make pastry with *cold* hands. I always wash mine in cold water before I begin. And Maman makes her pastry on a marble slab."

"Cold hands—I've got that down. Now, carry on."

"Well, here is a good recipe for SHORT PASTRY that is not too rich:

ONE LB. OF PLAIN FLOUR

HALF LB. OF FAT—BUTTER IS BEST, BUT LARD OR MARGARINE
   WILL DO
PINCH OF SALT
COLD WATER

Cut your fat into small pieces, and rub as lightly as you can into the flour, into which you should have sifted your salt. Flour your fingers well, and rub the fat between them, doing it with your hands about ten to twelve inches above the bowl until it is all crumby. Add a little baking powder—not much, though. Have cold water ready in a jug, and add a little at a time, mixing with a knife—never a fork—until you have a stiff dough. You must be very careful not to get it too wet, or you will spoil your pastry. Sprinkle flour over your baking-board, and turn the pastry on it, running a knife round the bowl to remove any that may have stuck. Then flour your rolling-pin, and roll *lightly* and *always from you*. Never roll backwards and forwards. You turn the cake round lightly with your fingers until it is even. Roll to about half inch in thickness for fruit tarts. If it is for a meat pie, it should be a little thicker, though—say three-quarters of an inch."

"Why?" demanded Jo.

"Because your meat pie should be rather more solid. Now that is the recipe. Shall I give you some ideas of how to use it?"

"Well, we ought to say something about that. Give us apple tarts. Yours really are delicious."

"Well, here is a good one for APPLE TART.

Line a sandwich tin with the pastry, and fill up either with apples which you have previously stewed to a pulp, or with the fruit grated or cut up very thinly. Add sugar to taste; and if you like a few cloves—say three or four—or a quarter of a spoonful of powdered cinnamon— No, Jo; we won't say anything about garlic."

"I never said a word!" retorted Jo aggrievedly.

"I saw it in your eye. Do you ever forget anything of the kind?"

Jo chuckled, but made no reply, and Simone went on:

"Cover your fruit with pastry, cut round the edges with a sharp knife to neaten, and prick two holes to allow the steam to escape. Bake in a hot oven—*never* put pastry into anything but a *hot* oven, mind!—at say 400 for electricity, or 8 for gas."

"Now it's my turn," said Marie. "I'll give you what Corney calls 'DEEP-DISH APPLE PIE'. She says it's always called that in U.S.A."

"I suppose the Puritans took the recipe over when they sailed in the *Mayflower*," said Jo.

"This is a *cookery* book, not a history one," Frieda reminded her. "Do go on, Marie! If we let Jo begin on history, we shall never get anything done, as you ought to know!"

"Oh, don't mind me!" replied Jo resignedly. "I'm ready."

"Very well. Put the title, and I'll begin."

Jo meekly scrawled the title, and then lifted her head.

"I'll begin with apples," said Marie briskly. "You use the same recipe for pie crust, so we needn't repeat it. Now:

"Shred your apples very finely. Put in a pastry support or an old egg-cup into your piedish. Either grease or wet the edge of the dish all round, and then fill up with the apple to which you can add cloves or cinnamon—and, of course, sugar. Fill the dish nearly to the top, and put in about two tablespoonfuls of water. Cut strips of the pastry, and line the rim of the dish with them. Wet the strips, lay the cake of your pastry over, and trim the edges. Prick holes for the steam, and bake in your hot oven."

"Now for other fillings," said Jo. "I'll begin this. Try gooseberries with just a pinch or two of cinnamon."

"I like red currants and raspberries," observed Simone. "But you would need no water with them as they are both juicy fruits."

"Blackberry and apple are good, too," was Frieda's contribution.

"What I like are cranberries," said Marie. "But they are so sour that you must use golden syrup to sweeten them."

"Actually, you can use any fruit this way," supplemented Simone.

"Quite true," said Jo. "Well, are we going to say anything about open tarts—or flans, don't *you* call them, Simone?"

"Yes; that is right. They are easy. You make your pastry case first by lining a deep sandwich tin. Put a sheet of grease-proof paper over your pastry, and some good-sized crusts of bread on top of that to keep it in position. Just when it is beginning to turn yellow, remove your crusts and paper to finish off. When they are cold, fill with fruit or jam, or if you want to cook your fruit, you can put it in when you remove the paper. But be careful not to burn it."

"It's my turn now," said Jo, as she had finished this. "I'm going to put in Apple Charlotte—which, incidentally, you can use with other fruits like the pies. Here goes:

APPLE CHARLOTTE

Thickly grease your piedish with butter or marge, and sprinkle this with sugar—brown is best if you have it handy. You can also use honey or golden syrup. Now put in a layer of soft white breadcrumbs; then a layer of stewed apple; then more breadcrumbs, and so on, until the dish is full. Finish off with a layer of breadcrumbs and sugar. Put a few dabs of your fat over all, and bake golden-brown in a moderate oven. This," added Jo, as she wrote, "is the sort of pudding most people make complete pigs of themselves over."

"And *now* who is finishing her sentences with prepositions, I'd like to know?" cried Frieda.

"Oh, well, 'over which', if you prefer it. Now, have we finished with apples?"

"No; I'm going to give you APPLE SNOW," said Marie. "It is quite easy, and it makes a very pretty pudding. Here you are, Jo:

"Stew some cooking apples in their skins with just a very little water, then put them through a sieve. Sweeten to taste, and let them grow cold. Then beat up the whites of two eggs until they stand up—and, by the way, always beat whites of eggs on a plate with a flat wire whisk. If you haven't one, use the blade of a knife. Stir the whites lightly into the apple, and beat again—also lightly. Turn out into a dish, and decorate with dabs of red-currant jelly. Serve very cold."

"That will do for apples," decided Jo. "We could go on, I know. Apples are such useful things, aren't they?—though Eve didn't exactly find them so."

"Perhaps not." Frieda spoke hurriedly, for there was a wicked glint in Jo's eyes, and there was never any knowing what she might take it into her head to say. "I agree with you that we have done enough about them. Suppose we go on to milk puddings now? I have a recipe for Crême Anglaise—what you call 'custard', Jo."

"That's easy enough!" quoth Jo. "Just shove some custard powder into a basin, stir with a little milk; boil the rest of the milk with some sugar and pour on, stirring all the time. Then pour the lot back into the pan, and simmer till it thickens. Very simple!"

"No—*no*—NO!" cried Frieda with horror. "That is not proper custard at all! Take this down, Joey, and never use any other recipe!"

Jo chuckled. "Brought up to scratch for once, Frieda, my love! I thought, somehow, you'd rise to that. All right; go ahead!"

Frieda cast her a despairing look. "*Jo!* You are the—the *limit*!"

"You ought to know me by this time, my dear! Now go on with the recipe. I'm all set and ready."

Frieda gave it up as a bad job, and proceeded.

BOILED CUSTARD

TWO EGGS—DUCK'S EGGS IF YOU CAN GET THEM

THREE TABLESPOONFULS OF SUGAR
ONE PINT OF MILK
A PINCH OF SALT
FLAVOURING

Put the milk to boil. Beat the eggs and salt and sugar to a rich foam. When the milk boils, pour it over the eggs, stirring well all the time. Pour into the upper half of a double boiler, or, if you have not one, another smaller pan set inside a saucepan of boiling water will do as well. Cook till it thickens, but stir all the time."

"Why not just pour it into the milk pan and cook it?" inquired Jo.

"Because, whatever happens, you must never let the custard boil. If you do, it will curdle. But if you do cook it in a pan, and it does come to the boil by accident, then put a tablespoonful of cold water into it, and pour into a cold dish at once."

"I see. On the whole, I think I'd prefer the double boiler method. It would certainly be safer. Oh, before I forget, why *duck's* eggs?"

"Because they give you a richer custard. Also, if you want a very rich one, you can add a third egg."

"I see. Well, is that all?"

"All but the serving. The prettiest way is to pour it into custard glasses, grate a little nutmeg over the top, and serve when cold either alone or with stewed fruit. But you can serve it in a large dish if you like. Or cut up some oranges or, indeed, any other fruit, and pour the custard over that. Then ornament it with grated coco-nut or those tiny coloured sweets—hundreds and thousands, don't you call them?"

"That would look pretty," said Marie. "Now it's my turn, and I'll give you my baked custard recipe. Take a fresh sheet of paper, Jo, and begin."

"I've got two lines left on this, and paper's a bit scarce in this place," protested Jo. "I say!" And her eyes widened. "Where did you get that?" For Marie had quietly produced a packet of foolscap, which she laid before the scribe.

"I saw you were running short, so I wrote to Wanda, and it came to-day. Now stop arguing, and get on, or we shall never finish. I know Simone's got something special she's bursting to give you, but we may as well finish with custards before we begin on something else."

"All right—Legree!"

"All right—*who*? What did you call me?"

"Legree, my child—Simon of that ilk. To be found in *Uncle Tom's Cabin*. I'll lend it to you when we go back, and you'll see what I mean all right, then. Won't you be pleased, though!"

"There's something horrid at the bottom of this," said Marie suspiciously. "We must get on; but I shan't let it rest there, I can tell you. Take up your pen, Joey. We'll settle about this Legree business later."

Neither of the other two having read the book, they were forced to bottle up their curiosity, though all were certain that Jo "meant something". Later on, when they found out the kind of character Mr. Simon Legree had been, they overwhelmed her with reproaches, but she remained quite unperturbed. However, at the moment, as she consented to go on with the writing, Marie settled down to dictate:

BAKED CUSTARD

Prepare this in the same way as for boiled custard, but pour into a buttered piedish, place in a very cool oven, and cook slowly until set. Some people set the piedish into another with water in it, and this makes a delicious custard. You can make a delightful sweet from it if you leave it for a day, and then cut it into squares. Beat up the yolk of an egg. Dip each piece in it and then into crushed ratafia biscuits, and fry very gently in butter. But I don't advise that for every day. It's a party dish."

"I should say it was," said Jo, as she finished. "By the way, Frieda, you said 'flavouring' in your recipe, but you didn't say what flavouring to use. What do you suggest?"

"The best is peach leaves," said Frieda; "just two or three. But if you cannot get them, then a few drops of almond essence is good. If you use peach leaves, you should remove them before serving the custard."

"Got that down! Now then, Simone, it's your turn. What's yours?"

Simone looked firmly at Jo, but there was mischief in her eyes. "Rice pudding," she said. "Nice rice pudding!"

"'There ain't no such animile,'" quoted Jo.

"Oh, yes, there is. You just try this, and you'll want a second helping."

"What'll you bet?"

"Nothing—knowing you! But take it down, and try it some day."

"I'll take it down; but I can't think of any way of cooking rice that'll make me like it."

Simone declined to argue. She merely dictated:

CREAMY RICE PUDDING

TWO OZ. OF RICE
SUGAR TO TASTE
FLAVOURING—some people like nutmeg, but you can use what you like
ONE PINT OF MILK
HALF TABLESPOONFUL OF SUET

Wash the rice in three or four different waters, and then put into a piedish, and just cover with water. Put this into the oven, and cook slowly until the rice has absorbed all the water. Then stir in the milk, flavouring, sugar, and suet. Bake very slowly for at least two hours, when it should come out a rich, creamy mixture. You can add raisins, currants, or any other dried fruits you like. And here is another way of serving it. Let your rice grow cold, then make a flan case and after beating up the rice with the yolk of an egg, fill your pastry with it, and bake in a moderate oven to a golden brown. It should be eaten cold."

"Well, thanks for the recipe," said Jo. "I might try it—*once*!"

"You do, and you'll never refuse it again. And now it's your turn. So far you haven't given us a recipe for a single pudding, except Apple Charlotte. What are you going to do about it?"

Jo thought. "Pancakes!" she said, with the air of one who is visited by a supreme inspiration.

"Pfannkuchen?" asked Frieda.

"Yes; but not quite like yours. Ours are not so solid." Jo gave a giggle as she said this, and was promptly beset by demands to know what was at the bottom of this.

"Only that one day, when Madge was in Innsbruck, she asked for one each for Bill and her—Bill was with her. She said the waiter gazed at her in frozen horror for a moment, and then said, 'One *each*?' Neither of them could think why he was so surprised, but they said yes, very haughtily, I gather. When he returned with the things, they nearly swooned at the sight. Madge said that *one* of them would have made a meal for half a dozen hungry men! And chockful of jam, too."

Frieda and Marie joined in her giggles. "No," said the former, when they had sobered a little. "Your pancakes cannot be the same if they asked for one each. Give us your recipe, Jo."

So Jo began:

PANCAKES

FOUR OZ. OF FLOUR

ONE EGG—OR ONE OZ. OF DRIED EGG

HALF PINT OF MILK—EITHER FRESH OR SOUR

Put the flour into a basin, make a hole in it, and break the egg into the hole. Then add the milk, little by little, beating all the time until it is absolutely smooth, and frothy. The more you beat it the better—like 'a woman, a dog, and a walnut tree', you know."

"We don't, but it's best not to interrupt at present," murmured Marie. "Go on, Jo."

"Well, when your mixture is ready, pour it into a jug. Now take your frying-pan—a smallish one for choice. Put a knob of butter in it, and set it over a moderate heat. When the smoke is rising blue, pour a little of your mixture into the pan—enough to make a thin skin. Personally," added Jo, "I turn the pan while I'm pouring, so that it skins evenly. Leave for a few seconds until it sets. Then slip a broad knife blade under it to prevent it sticking. Let it brown, and then turn with your knife, and brown on the other side. Sprinkle with sugar and a few drops of lemon juice, if you like lemon, roll, and set on a hot dish in the oven or over a pan of boiling water to keep hot while you fry the rest. Voilà tout!"

"But," said Simone, "that is almost the same as our CRÊPES SUZETTES. The only difference is that when the pancakes are done, you pour a liqueur over them, and set fire to them to crisp them."

"It sounds distinctly extravagant," said Jo. "As this book is intended for girls like us, I think we'll leave that. What next?"

"We should give one or two steamed puddings, I think," said Marie. "I remember Frau Mieders' foundation recipe. Shall we put that in? You can do so much with it by altering the flavouring."

"A very good idea," agreed Frieda. "Put it in, Joey."

"Well, as it'll save us a lot of trouble, I think we will," said Jo. "It's a good thing you know it, Marie, for I'm never very sure of quantities in this."

"Oh, I know it," said Marie confidently. "Take it down, Jo.

STEAMED PUDDINGS: FOUNDATION RECIPE

TWO OZ. FAT
TWO OZ. SUGAR
FOUR OZ. FLOUR
ONE EGG
A LITTLE MILK
HALF TEASPOONFUL BAKING POWDER

Beat the fat and sugar together until they are light and creamy. Then beat your egg thoroughly, and add it gradually with alternate spoonfuls of the flour. *Do not beat once you begin adding flour—only stir gently.*"

"Why?" demanded Jo.

"Because if you beat your mixture will become a batter, and you want a sponge. Add the milk to this, and sour milk will do as well as fresh. Grease a basin of medium size, and pour in. By the way, your mixture must not fill the basin, for this is a pudding that should rise a good deal. If you want something more than a plain sponge pudding, put lemon or orange curd, jam, currants, or marmalade in the basin and then add the mixture. Cover with a large sheet of grease-proof paper, and tie it with a string. Place in a steamer over a pan of boiling water and steam for two hours. Be sure your water is boiling before you put the pudding in. If you haven't a steamer, set the basin in boiling water about two-thirds up it. If you have made a plain pudding, you can serve with boiled custard or syrup. And you can vary the pudding by putting dates or any other kind of dried fruit into the mixture. Or you can make it a chocolate pudding by adding 2 oz. of cocoa to the flour."

"In short, a good, useful, all-the-year-round recipe," finished Jo.

"I've often thought so," acknowledged Marie. "Now, what next?"

"A little rest and refreshment, I should say. My wrist is aching." And Jo rubbed her wrist gently.

"Poor old lady!" laughed Marie. "I'll go and see what I can scrounge." She left the room, to return presently with big glasses of creamy milk and little tarts made of Blaubeeren—the blue berries which, in England, as Jo remarked, are called bilberries, wimberries, or blaeberries. The girls were all fond of them, so Marie's tray was greeted with a cheer.

"The only trouble is," said Jo, when she had finished her share, "that they do make your mouth blue. Look at my teeth!" And she grinned on them with teeth that were distinctly purplish.

"You can always wash your teeth," said Frieda soothingly. "And yours are no worse than ours. Jo! Do stop grinning like that! You look like a—a—"

"A cannibal surveying his fellowmen, and wondering which will be the juiciest and most tender for the pot," finished Marie.

"Well, I think a touch of the old toothbrush is indicated. *And* my fingers are sticky. I'm off to wash!" And Jo departed upstairs, whistling like a blackbird as she went. The rest were not slow to follow her, and presently they were all once more round the table, with teeth restored to their normal colour. Simone had taken the tray to the Küche, and on returning, volunteered the information that it looked like clearing up at last, so they had better get on and finish their pudding recipes in case they were able to go out after Mittagessen.

"All right," said Jo. "I feel better now. What shall we do next? Suet pudding, since we're on boiled and steamed?"

"Do you know the recipe?"

"I do; so I'll be responsible for it."

And she wrote:

SUET PUDDING

FOUR OZ. OF PLAIN FLOUR
ONE TEASPOONFUL OF BAKING POWDER
A PINCH OF SALT
TWO OZ. OF SHREDDED OR MINCED SUET
TWO OZ. OF WHITE BREADCRUMBS

Mix all the ingredients in a basin, rubbing the suet well in. Moisten with water or milk to a stiff dough. It is best to mix with an old sharp knife. Turn out on to a floured baking-board, and roll out. Cut off enough to make a top for the pudding, roll the rest a little thinner, and line a greased basin in one piece. Add your filling, put on the top, and steam for two or three hours. This is another good recipe, for you can use almost any kind of cookable fruit for the filling. Apples, cherries, plums, damsons, blackberries—or Blaubeeren. And black currants are luscious!"

"I can give you a lovely recipe for apple pudding," said Frieda.

"Carry on, then," said Jo amiably.

APPLE PUDDING

Before lining the basin," began Frieda, "grease it heavily, and then sprinkle brown sugar or a little syrup over it. Then line it. Fill up with apple and sugar to sweeten—cloves or cinnamon to flavour. Add a little water, and then put on the lid. When it is done and you turn it out, it has the most delicious caramel coating."

"I must try that," said Jo greedily. "I love caramel!"

"And another thing," put in Marie, "you can roll out your paste, and spread it with jam or syrup, and then roll it up, wrap it in grease-proof paper, and put on a plate before you set it into the steam, and it makes a lovely roly-poly."

"Well, I think we've had enough sensible puddings. Let's have a few frivolous ones," suggested Jo. "What about a cream or two? Or a trifle?"

"I'll give you my Blackberry Fluff," said Simone eagerly.

"That topping thing we had at Abendessen the other night? Oh, let's have it! I meant to ask you for the recipe," agreed Jo.

She wrote:

BLACKBERRY FLUFF

ONE PINT OR ONE LB. OF BLACKBERRIES
QUARTER CUP OF SUGAR
ONE DESSERTSPOONFUL OF POWDERED GELATINE
HALF CUP OF WATER
HALF TABLESPOONFUL OF LEMON JUICE
WHITES OF TWO EGGS, STIFFLY BEATEN

Boil the blackberries, sugar, water, and lemon juice in a pan. When they have come to the boil, add the gelatine, dissolved in a little water. Strain the mixture through a sieve, and allow to cool until it begins to set. Beat up the whites of the eggs till quite stiff, and then mix thoroughly with your jelly. Turn all this into a dish, and put in a cool place to set. If you put it into a mould, don't forget to soak your mould thoroughly with cold water first. When you turn it out, you can serve it with boiled custard, or whipped cream, if you can get it. Alternatively, if you can spare the eggs, beat up the white of one egg with sugar till it is stiff, and put in spoonfuls round the jelly. It is very delicious, and makes a very pretty dish. And you can vary this, too, by using any kind of *soft* fruit that is in season: rasps, strawberries, currants—all of these do well. Now it's Frieda's turn."

"Well," said Frieda, "I am going to give you

QUINCES AND BAKED ORANGES

Peel and quarter the quinces, and stew them gently with sugar to taste. Remember that sometimes they take a long time to get soft. If you hurry them, you may spoil your dish, so no impatience, Jo, if you try this!"

"I like that! Am I the only impatient person in this outfit?"

"No; but you are dreadfully impatient in cooking."

"Well, I like to see something for my work *soon*," explained Jo.

"Well, remember what I say. The quinces may soften quite quickly. On the other hand they may not, and they *must* be soft for this."

"Oh, all right. If I ever try it, I'll be patient. Now go on."

"Put in a buttered baking-dish as many whole oranges as you want together with the quince quarters. Cover all with the quince syrup, and bake in a moderate oven until the oranges are tender. Then serve."

"Since we seem to be on fruit recipes," said Marie, "here is Pears and Chocolate Sauce."

"That sounds good," said Jo thoughtfully.

"It is. Write it down, Joey.

PEARS AND CHOCOLATE SAUCE

Use China pears for this if you can; but they are another fruit that take a long time to prepare. Put them in an earthenware jar, and bake in the oven with a little water. They should go pink when cooked in this way. Set them aside when done to grow cold. Then pour over them your chocolate sauce which you make thus:

> TWO OZ. OF BUTTER
> ONE OZ. OF FLOUR
> HALF PINT OF MILK
> SUGAR TO TASTE
> A FEW DROPS OF VANILLA ESSENCE, AND
> A TABLESPOONFUL OF GRATED CHOCOLATE OR COCOA

Melt half the butter in a saucepan, and add the flour. Cook for a minute or two, and then add the chocolate or cocoa—whichever you are using. Stir with a wire whisk, and make sure there are no lumps. Then add the rest of the butter by degrees, and when all is melted, add the vanilla, and pour over your cold pears. And for a really partyish affair," wound up Marie, "put your pears on vanilla ice cream, and the hot sauce over the lot!"

"Why can't we have a party at once?" wailed Jo. "I call this a most seductive recipe. I'm going to give you Grannie's Caledonian Cream, but it hasn't a thing on this, delicious though it is. Here you are.

CALEDONIAN CREAM

>WHITES OF TWO EGGS
>TWO TABLESPOONFULS OF RASPBERRY JAM
>OR
>TWO TABLESPOONFULS OF RASPBERRY PURÉE—SWEETENED

Beat the whites with a pinch of salt till they are stiff enough to stand up. Then beat in the jam or purée until the mixture is thick and fluffy. Serve in custard glasses. By the way, you can use it as a filling for sponge layer cake, too. It's what we generally give the babies for a birthday cake."

"It sounds quite as nice as any of ours," said Marie. "When I get home, I'm going to try it out at once. Now, Simone; what about you?"

"Well, I think I'll give you one kind of coffee cream," said Simone. "It's called

MOKKA-JOKKA

>HALF PINT OF STRONG BLACK COFFEE
>HALF PINT OF MILK
>TWO TABLESPOONFULS PLAIN FLOUR
>ONE TABLESPOONFUL BUTTER OR MARGARINE
>ONE TABLESPOONFUL GOLDEN SYRUP

Boil the milk with two or three drops of vanilla. Mix the flour, sugar, and cold black coffee together until there are no lumps in it. When the milk boils, pour it on the flour and coffee, and stir well. Return the whole mixture to the saucepan, and simmer till it thickens, stirring all the time. Add the butter and syrup. Boil a few minutes longer, then pour into a well-soaked mould, and leave to set."

And there they had to end, for Frau Winkelstein appeared, demanding the table for Mittagessen, and they had to clear it. Jo vowed her wrist ached as though it would break, but when she came to read over what they had done that morning, she agreed that it had been worth it.

"All the same," she added darkly, as they streamed upstairs to make themselves tidy before the meal, "Legrees, every one of you!"

CAKES, BISCUITS AND SWEETS

CAKES, BISCUITS AND SWEETS

THE weather cleared up enough for the girls to go for a long walk in the afternoon, and it was nearly four o'clock when they got back. Much too late for any more cookery book, Jo decreed, so they spent the rest of the evening after Abendessen in writing letters.

"But there isn't much more time left before we go home," said Jo, as they went upstairs to bed, "so we must get on to-morrow. I vote we do cakes. I don't know what else there is left after that."

"We'll do the cakes first, and then see what else we want to add," said Frieda, as she and Marie turned in at the room they shared. Jo and Simone were on the other side of the landing. They parted, and no more was heard from any of them that night, though Marie declared at Frühstück next morning that she dreamed that Jo, after looking round them all, had seized on her and said she would make lovely Marie soup which they could eat with Marie biscuits.

"I never stirred out of bed!" said Jo indignantly.

"Oh, I don't mean you really did it," said Marie. "I only *dreamt* it. But it was very horrible. You would grin at me, and your teeth were sapphire blue, and glistened like a row of little lamps."

The shout of laughter with which the other three greeted this might have startled any listener. Frau Winkelstein, however, had known them all for some years now, and was accustomed to them, so she merely shrugged her shoulders, decided that quarantine or no quarantine, die jungen Damen were enjoying themselves, and left it at that.

When the meal was over and their chores done, they all gathered in the little Saal again, prepared to make the most of yet another rainy morning, and finish a cakes section of their book if they could.

"How should we begin this?" asked Jo.

"By giving a few general hints first, I think," said Frieda. "For instance, I am going to say that though one *can* make cakes with egg powder and margarine, the results are never so good as when one uses butter and fresh eggs."

"Well, *I* am going to say that before ever you begin to *make* the cakes, it is wisest to have everything ready: your tins greased, all the materials at hand, and egg-whisk, hair sieve, fork, knife, everything that you may need, before you," said Simone, with a severe look at Jo, who was always a sinner in this direction.

"I'm going to put in that you should always use plain flour," said that young lady quickly. "You can always add baking powder if you need it; but some cakes only require beating—"

"Yes!" interrupted Marie. "I forgot yesterday. What was that nonsense of yours about women and dogs?"

"Women and dogs?" repeated Jo, completely fogged for the moment.

"Yes; when we were talking of beating being good for batter mixtures."

"Oh, *that*! It's just an old English saying." Jo solemnly quoted:

> "A woman, a dog, and a walnut tree,
>   The more you beat them the better they be.

Dates from the Dark Ages, I should think; but I've heard it from my infancy, alas!" And she heaved an elderly sigh.

"I don't like it at all!" cried Frieda. "What a horrid saying! And I thought all you English were so fond of dogs!"

"Well, *I* didn't invent it. I don't agree with it at all," said Jo with emphasis. "But you wanted to know, so I've told you. Now, let's get on with our cakes. Marie, what hints are you going to give?"

"I am going to say never use either stale butter or eggs. And if you use more than one egg, break each separately into a cup and see that it is all right before you add it to the others, which should be poured into a basin, ready for beating. Otherwise, either you may spoil your cake by having a nasty egg in it; or else you waste what you've already broken."

"And here is another hint," said Simone, when they had all applauded Marie's hint. "Never bake large cakes in a hot oven; nor small ones in a cool."

"Here's my last effort. Do *not* forget the cake, once it's in the oven! Otherwise you may find it frizzled to a frazzle when you finally remember it. And there's all your work thrown away, to say nothing of your materials," quoth Jo.

"Well, you *should* know," murmured Frieda; whereat the other two shouted, for Jo was famed for committing this very fault.

"Shall we give Frau Mieders' general recipe?" asked Simone, when they were grave again—Jo had joined in the laughter, being well accustomed to being teased about her cooking exploits—and the secretary had picked up her pen once more.

"May as well," agreed Marie. "It's a good one. You give it, Simone."
"Very well. Are you ready, Jo? Then we'll call it:

CAKES: FOUNDATION RECIPE

FOUR OZ. OF BUTTER
FOUR OZ. OF SUGAR
TWO EGGS
SIX AND A HALF OZ. OF FLOUR
THREE-QUARTER TEASPOONFUL OF BAKING POWDER
TWO TO THREE TABLESPOONFULS OF MILK

Beat the butter to a cream with a wooden spoon. Add grated lemon or a few drops of orange juice, then the sugar, and beat again. The more you beat, the lighter your cake will be. Add slowly the well-whisked eggs, and beat thoroughly between each addition. Stir in lightly one-third of the flour—it is best to sift it as you add it. Sieve the remaining flour with the baking powder and stir that in; add flour and milk alternately. This mixture will be enough for a 6-inch cake tin. Line this with grease-proof paper, fire it and bake in a moderate oven—250–300 electricity, and 5–6 regulo—for 1½ hours. This mixture," continued Simone, "is a very useful one, for it can be varied so."

"Indeed it can," agreed Frieda. "If you put in glacé cherries it will make cherry cake."

"I made it at home just before we came away, and added three tablespoonfuls of cocoa to the eggs before putting in the flour," said Marie. "It makes a most delicious chocolate cake."

"Or two teaspoonfuls of carraway seeds gives you seed cake, and I really do have a weakness for seed cake," put in Jo. "I could eat a good-sized slice of seed cake this minute."

"It isn't nearly time for 'elevenses', so you must wait," Marie warned her. "But Wanda makes it, and puts in chopped preserved ginger, and a tablespoonful of the ginger syrup, and it makes a really luscious ginger cake."

"And if you use orange juice instead of milk, and the grated rind of an orange, you have a delightful orange cake," Simone added her quota. "Or dried fruit, and you have your favourite fruit cake, Jo. It really is a most excellent foundation."

Jo had been scribbling busily. Now she looked up. "I've put all that down. Hadn't we better get on to something else now? What about my own special gingerbread?"

"Oh, yes; we must have that!" cried Marie. "I shall have to ration Eugen with it when *I* make it. He ate four large slices of the last one you made, Jo! Did you notice? I was so ashamed."

"Bless the lad! It does my heart good to see him enjoy his food!" returned Jo, with her most grandmotherly air. "All right, Marie; I'll put it in, especially on his account, and you can tell him so."

She bent her head over the paper, and began aloud:

GINGERBREAD

TWELVE OZ. FLOUR
TWO TEASPOONFULS GROUND GINGER
HALF TEASPOONFUL BICARBONATE SODA
QUARTER LB. CASTOR SUGAR—though brown sugar is even better
TWO OZ. CANDIED LEMON PEEL
ONE TEASPOONFUL VINEGAR
TWO OZ. PRESERVED GINGER
QUARTER LB. BUTTER OR MARGARINE
HALF LB. OF TREACLE
TWO EGGS
HALF GILL MILK
ONE OZ. SPLIT ALMONDS

Sieve the flour, ground ginger, and bicarb. Add the sugar, peel, and preserved ginger. Put the butter and treacle into a saucepan, and melt gently. Beat the eggs, and add the milk and vinegar. Mix the treacle and butter with the flour, and then add eggs and milk. Stir these ingredients very thoroughly. Line a baking tin with greased paper, and pour in the mixture. Spread it evenly, and place the almonds, which should be blanched, here and there over it. Bake in a moderate oven for 1½ hours. When cold, put it away for four or five days."

"And then cut it and eat it," added Simone rapturously. "Don't you sometimes ice it, Joey? Has the icing a special recipe?"

"Yes; here you are:

> HALF LB. ICING SUGAR
> ONE TEASPOONFUL OF BUTTER
> A LITTLE BOILING WATER—SAY ONE TABLESPOONFUL
> COLOURING AND FLAVOURING

Melt the butter in the boiling water, and pour it on the icing sugar very gradually, so that you do not get it runny. Add your colouring and flavouring, and stir. Then spread over the cake, using a palette knife to smooth it. Decorate with crystallised ginger and almonds."

"Well, it's a very good cake," said Frieda.

"So good," Marie laughed, "that Eugen wanted to know, if you please, if we couldn't have an extra large loaf baked for the wedding feast. When I said one didn't have cakes like that at a wedding table, he asked if Jo wouldn't make one for us to take on our honeymoon."

"No, indeed Jo won't," cried that young lady loudly. "But if you two will let me into the secret of where the honeymoon is to be spent, I'll promise faithfully to send at least two to you while you're away. Is it a bargain, Marie?"

"Yes; if you can get Eugen to tell you," retorted Marie, who knew well enough that her bridegroom elect stood in mortal terror of Jo's tricks, and would even forego his beloved gingerbread on such conditions.

Jo knew this, too, so she chuckled, and then turned to Frieda. "Your turn, Frieda. What is your choice to be?"

"I'll give you Heidelberg cake. It is fairly easy, and *very* nice."

"I know it," said Jo feelingly. "It's a real cut-and-come-again cake. Just the thing to have in a family!"

HEIDELBERG CAKE

ONE OZ. YEAST
ONE LB. VIENNA FLOUR
EIGHT OZ. SULTANAS
ONE OZ. CURRANTS
TWO OZ. SUGAR
ONE TEASPOONFUL SALT IN A GILL OF WARM WATER
ONE GILL TEPID MILK

"Do you mean *two*-gills-one-pint, or *four*-gills-one-pint?" demanded Jo. "It makes a difference, you know."

"Oh, four gills. If your dough is too dry, you can always add a little more liquid. Put your yeast into the salt and water, and when it is melted, stir in the flour, sugar, fruit, and milk. Mix thoroughly together, roll into a ball, and place in a pan near the fire, and cover. Leave till it has risen to nearly as much again.

Then roll your dough out into a square. Glaze it with the yolk of an egg, thoroughly beaten, set on a tin, and bake in a moderate oven. When it is done and cold, cut into small squares."

"Guaranteed filling and wholesome, and most inviting," added Jo.

"You're not putting *that* in, I hope?" cried Frieda.

"Keep calm! That was just an addition for our noble selves. Now it's your turn, Simone."

"Well, I had thought of giving you BABAS, but as the mixture is very much the same as our foundation one, I'll just add that you grease your patty pans if you cannot get them castle-pudding shape. Then brush them over with a little raspberry jam before filling them. When the cakes are baked, turn them out, and dust with finely grated coco-nut. If you have any glacé cherries at hand, cut each into three pieces, and set one piece in the centre of each cake. That is all."

"No, Marie. You're the last; and then I've two or three recipes I simply must give you. After that, what about putting in one or two sweets, such as fudge?"

"Rather!" said the bride-elect. "If we are a great deal at the castle, it won't always be easy to get sweets, so I shall be glad to make them myself. I can't bear to be without sweets."

"Sugar baby!" laughed Jo. "Very well. Give us your cake recipe, and I'll finish off mine, and then we'll proceed to sweets. But I hope you and Eugen aren't going to live year in and year out up there in the mountains. It's a lovely place, I know; but we shall want to see something of you, even if you *are* married and done for!"

Marie protested at this, while the others shouted with laughter. However, she was calmed down, and persuaded to add her quota which was:

SAND CAKE

HALF LB. OF BUTTER OR MARGARINE
QUARTER LB. OF BLANCHED AND POUNDED ALMONDS
GRATED PEEL OF HALF A LEMON
SIX OZ. OF FLOUR
TWO TABLESPOONFULS SUGAR
THREE EGGS OR THE EQUIVALENT IN EGG POWDER
A LITTLE MILK

Cream the butter, and add the rest of the material in the order I've given them," said Marie. "Beat the eggs thoroughly before you add *them*, of course. When everything is thoroughly mixed, divide into three pieces and roll them out. Spread the first with marmalade or some other preserve, and put the second on it. Do the same with the second, and put the third on that. Set in a tin, and put into a slow oven. When it is half-baked, pour over it a water icing, return to the oven, and finish baking. Here is the recipe for WATER ICING:

QUARTER LB. OF ICING SUGAR
HALF GILL OF WATER
A LITTLE LEMON JUICE

Be sure your sugar is free from lumps. Mix the juice and the water together, and beat until thoroughly mixed. It should be rather thinner than ordinary white icing, as it has to be poured over, so if it is too thick, add a little more water, a teaspoonful at a time."

"And very good it sounds! That is one I shall certainly try," said Simone. "Why have you never told us before, Marie?"

"I suppose because I didn't think of it. We often had it when we lived in Wien. Our old Gretchen used to make it at least once a week because the boys and Papa were so fond of it. Now, Joey, what are your other recipes?"

Jo leaned back in her chair. "About a hundred years ago—more or less—a great English actor called Baddeley died and left a sum of money to Drury Lane Theatre to provide a Twelfth Night cake for whatever company was playing there. They still keep up the custom. The leading man cuts the cake, and everyone drinks to the health of Mr. Baddeley, and then they eat their cake. Here is the recipe—again more or less. You can use it for Christmas cake or birthday cake too. It's quite rich enough!" and after this, Jo took up her pen, and wrote:

TWELFTH DAY CAKE

HALF LB. OF BUTTER
HALF LB. OF CASTOR SUGAR
FOUR LARGE EGGS——DUCK IF POSSIBLE

ONE LB. OF CURRANTS OR RAISINS

SIX OZ. MIXED PEEL CHOPPED FINE

TWO OZ. GROUND ALMONDS

HALF TEASPOONFUL GRATED NUTMEG

ONE TEASPOONFUL MIXED SPICE

ONE LARGE TABLESPOONFUL OF RUM OR RAISIN WINE

TEN OZ. FLOUR

ONE LUCKY CHARM OR SILVER COIN FOR LUCK

Cream the butter, add the sugar, and cream again. Put in one egg at a time, beating hard. Add one-third of the flour sieved. Mix in the fruit, almonds, and spices, and moisten with your rum or whatever you are using. Stir in the remaining flour, and when it is well mixed, add your charm. Put the mixture into an 8-inch tin lined with greased paper. Bake for three hours in a moderate oven. When done, leave for two or three days. Then cover with almond icing, and allow it to stand for a further two or three days. Cover with royal icing. And that's all. Then you eat it."

"I dare say!" said Simone. "What about the icing recipes?"

"Icing is something I never make myself. Can't you give us any?"

"I'll give you a very good royal icing. Perhaps Marie or Frieda could give us the almond?" And Simone looked questioningly at them.

"Oh, I'll give you an almond icing recipe," returned Frieda readily.

"Then as that goes on first, we'd better begin with it," said Jo.

"Here is Mamma's recipe, then. You know how good that is." And Frieda gravely dictated:

ALMOND ICING

ONE LB. OF GROUND ALMONDS
HALF LB. SIEVED ICING SUGAR
HALF LB. CASTOR SUGAR
TWO SMALL EGGS
JUICE OF ONE LEMON
TWO TEASPOONFULS—ONE EACH OF ROSE WATER AND ORANGE-FLOWER WATER
QUARTER TEASPOONFUL ALMOND ESSENCE

Put the almonds and all the sugar into a basin, and rub well together with the finger-tips. Whisk the eggs thoroughly, and add. Stir a little and then put in the lemon juice and the flavourings. Mix well, and knead until a smooth ball is formed. Next take your cake, and look for any burnt parts. You must cut those off. Brush away any loose crumbs, and then paint the cake lightly and evenly with the slightly beaten white of an egg. Put the ball of icing on top of the cake and press it down evenly with your hands, finishing off with a rolling-pin. Cover the sides, and straighten the edges with a palette knife. Be sure it is evenly distributed over your cake. Leave two or three days to dry. Then you are ready for Simone's royal icing."

And Frieda nodded at Simone, who began at once:

ROYAL ICING

> ONE LB. FINELY SIEVED ICING SUGAR
> WHITES OF THREE EGGS
> A FEW GRAINS SCRAPED FROM THE WASHING-BLUE
> HALF TEASPOONFUL OF ACETIC ACID

Whisk the whites slightly, and add the icing sugar gradually, beating well until at least half has been put in. Add the blue and the acid, and beat very thoroughly, continuing to add the rest of your sugar till it is all used up and you have a smooth icing. Then spread this over the cake thinly with your palette knife, which you should dip frequently into boiling water. If you have an icing bag, you can add points and other designs if you like. But," finished Simone, "I don't advise anyone to try that until she can manage to get a smooth covering. It is not an easy thing to do well."

"Suppose you want coloured icing?" demanded Jo.

"That, too, is difficult. You must add only a drop or two of your colouring at a time, and beat hard with each addition until it is evenly spread throughout all the icing. Otherwise, you get a patchy effect."

"Well, so much for cakes," said Jo briskly. "Now I'm going to give you a recipe for scones, because they are useful things if someone comes along unexpected-like, and you haven't any cake in the house to offer them."

"How is that?" asked Frieda.

"Well, you can serve them hot out of the oven. And they don't take very long to make either. Oh, and while I think of it, remember that though they are spelt '*sco-nes*', they are called '*sconns*'!"

"Your language is so odd," complained Marie. "You have such strange spellings, and then you pronounce the words differently!"

"Can't help it," said Jo austerely. "That's how it is. Here goes:

SCONES

HALF LB. PLAIN FLOUR
HALF TEASPOONFUL BICARB SODA
ONE TEASPOONFUL CREAM OF TARTAR
QUARTER TEASPOONFUL SALT
ONE TEASPOONFUL CASTOR SUGAR
TWO OZ. BUTTER OR MARGARINE
MILK TO MAKE A FAIRLY SOFT DOUGH

Mix the dry ingredients together thoroughly, and then rub in the fat with your finger-tips. Add the milk, and stir in with a knife to a softish dough. Roll it out on a floured board to ½ inch thick, and cut in rounds with a cutter. Brush the scones over with milk, and put on a greased, hot, baking tin into a hot oven. Bake until well-risen; then lower the heat, and leave until golden-brown. Split, butter, and serve on a hot plate. If you want them cold, serve them in a folded table-napkin. You can also eat honey, jam, or marmalade with them. And if you want to use up some sour milk, you can use that, but in that case, put in only half the cream of tartar."

"It sounds thoroughly delicious," said Marie with approval. "Now, before we begin on the sweets, I want to put in my recipe for biscuits. Here you are:

BISCUITS

HALF LB. OF FLOUR
SIX OZ. BUTTER OR MARGARINE
FOUR OZ. CASTOR SUGAR
TWO OZ. RICE FLOUR
QUARTER TEASPOONFUL SALT
YOLK OF ONE EGG

Warm the butter, but do not oil it. When it is soft, add the sugar, and cream well. Beat in the yolk of the egg. Sieve the flour with the rice flour and salt, and add, mixing to a soft paste. Put the paste into a cool place for one hour. Then roll out on a floured board to half an inch in thickness. Cut out rounds or oblongs, and put on a baking tin lined with greased paper, and prick with a fork. Bake them in a moderate oven until golden-brown. When cooked, lift them off with a palette knife, and set on a cake-wire to cool. Pack into an air-tight box."

"That all?" asked Jo. "Good! I hear 'elevenses' coming, and I'm more than ready for it, I can tell you! This writing down of recipes is hungry work—especially when they are all so more-ish."

"So—*what*?" demanded Simone, to whom this was new.

"More-ish, my love. You know, 'Pass the plate again, please', that sort of thing! Oh, cheers! Hot chocolate and fancy bread! Frau Winkelstein, you're a queen of landladies! How is the mumpy one to-day?"

"Kurt is much better," said his mother, with a smile. "The lumps are vanishing, and he enjoys his food. He is longing to get up and go out to play, but that must not be yet. Now I will leave you to eat your little meal. Guten Appetit!" And with a smiling nod all round, she left them.

"My first attempt at sweets," said Jo, when the door had closed on the buxom form of Frau Winkelstein, "was butterscotch. My sister and brother used to make it on the dining-room fire when I was quite a small kid; and one fine day, they let me try. It was quite good, but it wasn't exactly butterscotch."

"The first thing I ever made," said Marie, "was fondants. Mamma mixed the fondant, that is, but she let me beat the colours into it and shape them. What fun it was!"

"I made nougat," sighed Simone. "My cousin, Marie-Andrée, used to come to stay with us for the New Year, and that was our treat."

"We did not make sweets," said Frieda. "Mamma was badly scalded with boiling sugar when she was a little girl, so she would never allow us to do anything of the kind. I had not made any till one Saturday at school, when we attempted toffee."

"Well, I vote we start off with good old butterscotch," said Jo, with her mouth so full that her words were indistinct.

"With *what*?" demanded Marie. "Your manners, Jo!"

Jo disposed of her mouthful. "I said butterscotch," she said. "Look here; it's pouring like mad. Let's write down the recipes now, and then make the sweets this afternoon, and send in a boxful for young Kurt. Hurry up, you people, and we'll begin."

"I've finished," said Marie, gulping down the last of her chocolate.

"So have I," chimed in Frieda.

Jo had already disposed of hers, so there was only Simone left. She looked at the impatient trio before her with a naughty sparkle in her eyes, and sipped her chocolate very deliberately. "I like to enjoy the flavour," she murmured.

But Jo was too much for her. Simone set down her cup for a moment, and her friend promptly snatched it up, shoved it on the tray, and picking that up, scuttled from the room, regardless of the French girl's lamentations.

"It serves you right," said Marie. "You might have guessed what Jo would do if you played like that. You *are* an ass, Simone!"

Jo returned a minute later, looking very pleased with herself, and sat down, pulled a fresh sheet of paper towards her, and headed it:

BUTTERSCOTCH

ONE AND A HALF CUPFULS GOLDEN SYRUP
SIX OZ. SUGAR
FOUR OZ. BUTTER
THREE DESSERTSPOONFULS VINEGAR
PINCH OR TWO OF SALT

Put all the ingredients into a saucepan, and stir until they are dissolved. Then simmer, still stirring, until a little of it forms a hard ball and 'cracks' when dropped into cold water. This is called the 'crack degree', or if you have a sugar thermometer—I haven't, by the way!—280 Fahrenheit. Add a few drops of vanilla essence, and pour into a shallow, well-greased tin to harden. While it is still warm, mark it into small squares, cutting rather deeply, and leave till quite cold before breaking up."

"If you made some to send away, would you send it as it is, or wrap each lump in paper?" asked Marie.

"I should say line your tin with grease-proof paper, and put in a layer, then a covering of grease-proof and another layer, and so on," said Jo. "It's sticky stuff, you know."

"True; so it is. Shall I give you our Russian caramel recipe?" asked Marie.

"Yes; do! They really are delicious! We'll make some this afternoon."

"Very well, then. Are you ready?

RUSSIAN CARAMELS

TWO OZ. BUTTER
ONE TABLESPOONFUL GOLDEN SYRUP
ONE DESSERTSPOONFUL CASTOR SUGAR
ONE TEASPOONFUL VANILLA ESSENCE
ONE TIN SWEETENED CONDENSED MILK

Any condensed milk will do," added Marie, "a half-pint tin. Oil the butter, and add golden syrup, sugar, essence, and milk, in that order, so be sure you get it down correctly, Joey. Cook over a *slow* heat, stirring all the time. When it is thick and a rich golden colour, and it has reached the 'hard ball' stage, pour into a greased tin, and cut into squares. When cold, the caramels should be wrapped in waxed paper, though grease-proof will do if you can't get waxed."

"Now, let's have your fondant recipe, Simone," said Jo. "It's quite the best I ever tasted, and fondant is the foundation for so many kinds of sweets, we must have it in."

Simone was inclined to be on her dignity after Jo's barefaced act of piracy with her chocolate, but she could not resist such an appeal, so she relaxed a little.

"I will give it to you, Jo. But it is not easy to make successfully, for it means hard work, and so many people have not the patience to go on with the beating. However, here it is:

FONDANT

TWO LB. GRANULATED SUGAR
TWO AND A HALF GILLS WATER
ONE TABLESPOONFUL GLUCOSE

By the way, you had better add that if you cannot obtain glucose, it will do to use one teaspoonful of cream of tartar. Dissolve the sugar in the water very, very slowly, until the last grain has disappeared. Then add the glucose or cream of tartar, whichever you are using; put on the lid, and boil up to 240 or 'soft ball' degree. When the bubbles have died down, pour the syrup into a large, earthenware basin—*never* use enamel!—which has been rinsed out with cold water. Leave till it is half-cold. Then take a wooden spoon, and beat the syrup till it turns, that is, becomes creamy and white. This takes a lot of doing, but it will not be fondant if it is not carried out. Besides, if you do it properly, your fondant will keep for weeks, wrapped in wax paper and not exposed to the air."

"How about flavouring and colouring?" inquired Jo meekly.

"That, too, needs care. You must add a drop or two at a time of each, and knead very thoroughly. First coat your hands with icing sugar, and then knead in the flavour before you add the colour. And you must be careful to see that both are spread throughout your ball. When it is ready, you pinch off little balls, and shape with your fingers. Mould the ball by rubbing in your hands. Then, instead of rolling round and round, roll up and down the palms two or three times, lay on your board or marble slab and press it gently so that the base becomes flat. You can make conical shapes by just pressing the round ball. If you can get some hazel nuts, peel and half them, and press a half on the top of a ball, or you can use almonds for ovals. To make peppermint creams, sugar your board and your fondant, roll out to half-inch thickness when you have flavoured it, and cut out little rounds about one inch in diameter. You can vary this as much as you like. With the vegetable dyes for cooking, you can tint your bonbons most lovely colours."

"Or," said Marie, "if you stone a date, and put fondant into the date instead, it makes a most delicious sweet."

"You can do that with French prunes, or figs," added Jo.

"What flavouring would you advise?" asked Frieda.

"Well, peppermint, vanilla, almond, lemon, orange-flower water, rose water, all make delicious bonbons. And you can get dyes to match. Keep peppermint white, of course, or pale green."

"And if you want to use them for a Christmas present," put in Marie, "cut some little squares of the paper one uses for lining shelves. Fold them from corner to corner four or five times, then open them, and you have a dear little crinkled case for your sweet. And you know what pretty boxes we make with wallpaper coverings. I call it a lovely present."

"One year," said Jo, "we—Madge and I, that is—made the duckiest Easter gifts for the babies this way. We coloured a little of the fondant yellow, and made it into wee ovals. Then we moulded some white fondant over the yellow, and melted some plain chocolate, and dipped them into it. They looked just like eggs. We made little plaited baskets, and filled them, and tied ribbons from old Christmas cards over them. The infants *were* thrilled! Especially when they cut them across, and saw the whites and yolks. That was a most successful Easter gift!"

"I'm sure it was!" agreed Frieda. "Well, is that the end?"

"Oh, I think so," said Jo.

"No, it isn't!" cried Marie. "We haven't said a word about fudge! You couldn't do a cookery book without giving a fudge recipe! I've got one you can have. Take it down, Joey!

FUDGE

ONE LB. GRANULATED SUGAR
ONE AND A HALF GILLS MILK
TWO OZ. PLAIN CHOCOLATE
ONE OZ. BUTTER
PINCH CREAM OF TARTAR

Scrape the chocolate, and dissolve it slowly with the sugar and milk in a pan over slow heat, stirring gently. Add butter and cream of tartar, and boil to 242 Fahrenheit—if you drop a little into cold water, it forms a soft ball. Take the pan from the fire, and beat the fudge with a wooden spoon. It will be stiff at first, and softens gradually. As soon as it loses its clear appearance, turn it out on a greased tin. When it is half-cold, cut into squares, and then leave to cool completely. If you don't want to make chocolate fudge, you can flavour the cream with a little black coffee, or vanilla, or ginger. Peanut butter may be used instead of ordinary butter."

"Anyhow, whatever you do about the flavouring, it's scrummy!" concluded Jo. "Well, that's all I'm going to write now. Here comes Posty, and he's got a whole package of letters, so there ought to be some for us. Come on, you folk!" And she led the race to the front door.

CHEESE DISHES

CHEESE DISHES

"CHEESE," said Frieda thoughtfully, "is very useful in cooking. One can make even simple things savoury with a cheese sauce. I feel that we should give a few cheese recipes, Simone. Don't you agree with me?"

Simone nodded. "Oh, I do! I have a most delicious recipe from Spain that someone gave Maman. It makes an excellent 'little' dish if one wishes a light meal; and yet it is satisfying."

"Very well," said Jo. "We'll go cheesy, and have a few cheese dishes. What shall we begin with?"

"Cheese sauce," said Marie. "That is what you use to pour over so many things—cauliflowers—"

"Potatoes or boiled beans," put in Frieda quickly.

"Oh, dozens of things," said Jo. "Well, Simone, you'd better give it seeing you come from the country of sauces. Begin!"

Simone laughed. "Very well.

CHEESE SAUCE

ONE TABLESPOONFUL OF PLAIN FLOUR

ONE TABLESPOONFUL OF FAT

HALF PINT OF MILK

A LITTLE MUSTARD AND CAYENNE PEPPER

THREE OZ. GRATED CHEESE

Make thick Béchamel sauce, but before adding your milk, sift the pepper and mustard with the flour. When the milk is added, and all well stirred together, add your cheese, and simmer, stirring all the time until the cheese is melted and thoroughly blended with everything."

"Any special cheese for this?" asked Jo.

"Parmesan is the best for cooking. And use old cheese to grate rather than new. New cheese is often soft and does not grate well."

"I'll just add that," said Jo, suiting the action to the word. "Now, who comes next?"

"You!" It was a spontaneous shout from the other three.

"Me? I'm doing the writing, and I've given you lots of recipes, anyhow," protested Jo. "Some folk are never satisfied!"

"You're going to be our author," Marie told her. "You must do your share."

"Yes; but I never, in my wildest moments, imagined I should try to become a second Mrs. Beeton!"

"It's a long way after your Mrs. Beeton," retorted Marie. "Her book is a veritable tome! This is just a little one for us, and girls like us."

"Oh, well; have it your own way. I'll give you Welsh Rarebit." And Jo screwed up her face, and wrote:

WELSH RAREBIT

> HALF LB. OF CHEESE GRATED
> HALF TEACUPFUL OF MILK
> YOLKS OF TWO EGGS
> SALT. MUSTARD. CAYENNE
> SLICES OF FRIED BREAD OR HOT, BUTTERED TOAST

Put the cheese and milk into a saucepan, and boil quickly, stirring all the time. Add the yolks well beaten, and the seasonings. Pour this mixture over the bread or toast, and brown under the griller. Serve very hot. Eggs can be omitted if wished."

"Now we'll have Simone's Spanish recipe," said Frieda, when Jo had finished this. "What is it, Simone?"

SPANISH RICE

> FOUR OZ. OF RICE
> TWO LARGE TOMATOES
> ONE OZ. OF BUTTER OR MARGARINE
> TWO TABLESPOONFULS OF GRATED CHEESE
> PEPPER AND SALT

Boil the rice, and drain well after you have added the pepper and salt. Melt the fat in a saucepan, put in rice, and fry until well browned. Slice the tomatoes, and add, stirring well. Cheese comes last, and you simmer all, stirring all the time, till the cheese is melted. Serve very hot, piled up on a dish."

"It sounds very good," said Frieda cordially. "Well, I shall give you a Macaroni Cheese dish.

NEAPOLITAN MACARONI CHEESE

Put 4 oz. of macaroni into a pot of boiling salt water, and cook till tender. Drain off, and wash in cold water. Make a cheese sauce—Simone's recipe will do—and add a teaspoonful of made mustard. Butter a shallow dish, and lay the macaroni in it; cover with the sauce and make a top with a layer of fine breadcrumbs and a thick layer of grated cheese. Bake in a moderate oven for 30 minutes or until it is a rich golden-brown."

"I've got Sicilian Sandwiches for you," said Marie mysteriously. "Warranted to give you shrieking nightmare if you eat them too late at night; but simply delicious, all the same."

"Then let's have it," said Jo. "I like the sound of it!"

SICILIAN SANDWICH

SLICES OF BREAD
TWO TABLESPOONFULS OF BUTTER

CHEESE DISHES

>THREE-QUARTER TEACUP OF GRATED CHEESE
>THREE TOMATOES
>THREE TABLESPOONFULS OF CHUTNEY
>SLICES OF BACON

Spread each slice of bread with butter, and cover with cheese thickly. Arrange slices of tomato over the cheese, and then spread with chutney. Place a slice of bacon on top of that, and put under the griller, and cook until the cheese is melted, and the bacon crisp."

"It sounds as hair-raising as a recipe I once heard," said Jo.

"What was that?"

"Not suited to this book. If ever we write another, I'll give it to you then. But I've done my share, and it's Simone's turn. It's no use teasing, Marie. I'm not going to give it to you now. We might want to do a second book, and then I should be sunk. I'll save it for that. I may say I've tasted it, and dreamed I was being chased by a spider with legs that were a yard long, all round the Tiern See afterwards. Come on, Simone!"

"You've had mine," said Simone. "It's either Marie again, or Frieda. Frieda, you haven't given us a single recipe yet. Do you not know one?"

"Two or three," said Frieda promptly. "The difficulty is to know which to give."

"Say them all over, and we'll choose what we like." This was Jo's modest suggestion.

Frieda shook her head. "I think not. I will give you Kaeser Liebesträume."

"How much? Cheese Love Dreams? They sound lurid!" said Jo. "Anyhow, I must put it into English as this is an English book. If it makes a real stir, it can be translated into other languages later. Come on! Let's have your Love Dreams!"

Frieda laughed, and then dictated

LOVE DREAMS

ONE OZ. OF MANGO CHUTNEY
TWO OZ. OF HAM OR BACON
TWO TABLESPOONFULS OF CHEESE
FOUR ROUNDS OF BREAD
A LITTLE CREAM, OR TOP OF THE MILK

Fry the bread. Make a paste of the ham by mincing or chopping it finely and moistening it with the cream. Spread the sandwiches with this paste and put a layer of chutney over it. Grate a thick layer of cheese over all, and bake or grill a light brown, and serve hot."

"All cheese dishes seem to need to be served hot," said Jo, as she finished this. "Marie, I've just remembered. We *must* have your recipe for making CREAM CHEESE OUT OF SPOILT MILK. It's such a saving of waste in hot weather, besides being quite delicious. How do you do it? I've often wondered."

"Oh, that's easy enough," said Marie. "Just strain the whey off your milk very carefully, so as not to break up the curds. Put the curds into a bag of double cheese-cloth or fine muslin, tie round, and hang up to drain for twenty-four hours. It depends on how you are going to use it when you come to flavouring. If you want to use it as a savoury, beat it up with salt and cayenne; make a pat, and sprinkle with chopped chives. I once tasted it sprinkled with finely minced sage. You can make a sweet of it by beating in sugar, and sprinkling with powdered cinnamon, or use it with just a little salt flavouring, spread on bread, and then add a thin skin of red-currant jelly."

"So that's how you do? Well, I'm very glad to know. I've always loved it when I've had it at your home. But, being a shy and modest violet, I never liked to ask for the recipe before," said Jo.

"Shy and modest? You!" cried Marie loudly.

"*Most* shy and modest," returned Jo firmly. "Frieda, while we *are* busy, what about that recipe of yours for cheese straws?"

"Of course!" said Frieda. "You do love them, don't you, Marie?"

"My love for them is nothing compared with Eugen's. I'm sometimes afraid I'm going to marry a very greedy man!" sighed Marie, with a quick glance down at the diamonds sparkling on her left hand. "Your cheese straws and Jo's gingerbread, and Simone's babas; he loves them all! I must certainly have your recipe, Frieda."

"What I wonder," said Jo, beginning to refill her pen, "is just *when* Marie is going to manage to do all this cooking. The Countess von und zu Wertheim isn't likely to have to cook for her family."

"You never know," said Marie solemnly. "There might be a war and we should have to fly and be refugees in another country. I should certainly want to be able to cook then! Eugen might even become poor. You can't be sure of anything nowadays."

"Only death and taxes, as Jem says," laughed Jo, referring to her brother-in-law, Dr. Russell. "Come along, Frieda; we'll have your cheese straws!" And she wrote:

CHEESE STRAWS

TWO OZ. OF BUTTER
TWO OZ. OF FLOUR
TWO OZ. OF BREADCRUMBS
TWO OZ. OF CHEESE
YOLK OF AN EGG

Mix the grated cheese, breadcrumbs, flour, and butter together with a little pepper and salt. Roll out and cut into thin strips. Bake them in a moderate oven to a light brown, and when done, pile them across each other.

"Well, that's easy to remember," she commented as she finished. "Two ounces of everything but egg. By the way, do you melt the butter?"

"Of course!"

"Well, you didn't say so. I'd better make a note."

"Now," said Simone, "I'll give you a cheese casserole to finish off. Are you ready, Jo? Then take this down.

CHEESE CASSEROLE

Cook some carrots, parsnips, turnips, potatoes, an onion, celery, or any other root vegetable you can find. Cold cauliflower is also good in this. Cut up your selection into small cubes. Butter a casserole and sprinkle it over with grated cheese. Fill the dish with the diced vegetables, and cover with a thick cheese sauce. Bake in a moderate oven for about quarter of an hour, and see that the top is a warm brown. Serve hot."

"Do you mean you use the lot or only some of these vegetables?" asked Jo doubtfully as she finished this.

"I dare say you could use them all if you liked; but there is no need. A choice of two or three would be quite enough. It is a very good way of using up left-over vegetables."

"Yes. Well, what about Abendessen? I feel rather like something left over myself at this minute," said Jo, shuffling her papers.

EGG DISHES

EGG DISHES

"WHAT do you think of first when eggs are mentioned?" asked Marie next day when the quartette were sitting round the table once more, ready to go on with their cookery book.

"Omelettes!" returned Simone promptly.

"I think of Easter and the Easter Hare," confessed Frieda, laughing.

"And I think of bacon and egg," wound up Jo. "I do love a bacon and egg brekker once in a while. As a rule, I prefer our coffee and rolls; but just every now and then I get a yearning for a good old English breakfast, and that's bacon and eggs every time. But the egg must be done just right—the white set firm, and the yolk just runny. It takes doing, I can tell you."

"How do you do it, then?" demanded Marie.

"Well, have your fat smoking hot; break the egg into a cup, and tilt your frying pan a little so that all the fat runs to one end. Pour your egg carefully into the fat, and then spoon the fat over the egg till it is done—that is, until the white covers the yolk. You should always add a pinch of salt to the egg before putting it into the fat. It helps to keep the yolk from breaking, and gives it a flavour."

"It sounds rather complicated," said Marie. "However, I've always enjoyed it when I've had bacon at the Sonnalpe. What comes next?"

"We had better have a recipe for poached eggs," said Simone. "I have one; here it is:

POACHED EGGS

The best way to do them is in a proper poaching pan; but if you haven't one, you can always poach an egg successfully if you have a small saucepan of boiling water, to which should be added a good pinch of salt. Break your egg into a cup, and *slide* it gently into the water, set the pan on a moderate heat, and boil until the white is set. Lift out with a fish-slice or a broad-bladed knife, and put on a slice of buttered toast. Serve very hot."

"What about boiled eggs?" asked Frieda. "You English seem to like your eggs boiled much harder than we do."

"Oh, you folk just let your eggs *look* at the water!" said Jo. "I hate eggs all runny. We do them in two ways. Either put them into boiling water, and boil from four to six minutes, according to the hardness you want your egg; or else put the egg into *cold* water, and bring to the boil, leaving on for one minute after the water is bubbling. This, by the way, is sometimes called 'Coddled Eggs'."

"Well, now it's my turn," said Marie. "I'm going to give you an omelette. It's just a foundation recipe. You can vary it by altering the seasoning to taste. Here you are, Joey. But first, I want to say that one should keep one pan for omelettes, and never allow it to be used for anything else. Well; what is it, Jo?"

"I was just remembering what happened to a *very* swagger omelette-pan Madge once had," she said demurely. "Oh, it wasn't *my* doing, for once! And I've said it first, you three, so you needn't even look it! Jem was experimenting with some herbal mixture of his own. He wanted a pan for boiling it, so he slipped into the kitchen, and picked what struck him as just the right thing: heavyish, flattish, and not too big. He finished his concoction, and then put the pan under a tap, swilled it round, wiped it with a tea-towel, and returned it to its shelf—all without even a squeak. Well, Madge decided to make an omelette for supper that night, and did so. Unfortunately," went on Jo blandly, ignoring the rising giggles of the others, "whatever that stuff of Jem's was, it was, shall we say, 'clinging' in flavour? Anyhow, that omelette tasted like no other omelette on this earth. Madge thought she was poisoned—and so did he! And the worst of it was that the pan was ruined so far as making omelettes in it was concerned. It *never* lost its flavour, and Jem had to buy Madge a new one. Then she kindly presented him with the other. He hasn't touched the household things for his experiments since. I'm only sorry," she added wistfully, "that I wasn't there to see their faces when they got good mouthfuls of that omelette!"

"You'd have been having a good mouthful yourself if you had, so I don't think you need to complain," said Marie, as well as she could between her peals of laughter. She pulled out her handkerchief and mopped her eyes. "Oh, dear! I'm aching! Well, shall I go on?"

Jo bent her head over her paper. "By all means," she said.

"Very well. A pan measuring about eight inches across is the best size, and it *should* be oval in shape. Put a large nut of butter or a spoonful of olive oil in your pan, and twist it about so that the fat runs all over, greasing the whole surface. Break your eggs, and separate the whites from the yolks. Beat up the whites till they are stiff, and the yolks to a thick froth. Add whatever flavourings you prefer to the yolks, and then stir lightly into the whites. Now, having got your pan thoroughly oiled and really hot, pour in the egg mixture. Leave for a few seconds, then slip a palette knife under the edges, and ease them up a little. The omelette will be brown underneath, though yellow and fluffy on top. If you want it like that, just double the omelette in two, slip on to a hot plate, and serve *at once*. If you prefer it, however, you can put the pan under a hot grill and brown the omelette on top. But the main thing to remember is that *all* omelettes should be eaten the moment they are cooked."

"What do you advise for flavourings?" asked Jo, pausing with her pen in the air.

They all tried to answer at once, but she shouted them down, and when she had got silence, she pointed at Marie, and said sternly: "One at a time, Marie. This is your recipe. Name a flavouring."

"Cheese grated finely," said Marie quickly.

"Asparagus tips," put in Frieda, "or you can use chopped roes or anchovy."

"Spinach purée is a good flavouring," added Simone, "and, of course, herbs of all kinds."

"Madge uses chopped ham for hers," said Jo. "Now, Simone."

"I'm going to give you the FRENCH WAY OF MAKING AN OMELETTE," said Simone. "In this, you break the eggs into a basin, and beat the yolks and whites together. Season with pepper and salt. Then add one teaspoonful of water, and whatever flavouring you have chosen. When your pan is hot and well greased, pour in the mixture, and keep shaking it and turning from side to side so that it sets evenly. Go on shaking and turning until all the egg is set. Then slide your palette knife under the edge, and turn over, and on to a hot plate. And I'm going to say what Marie did: you *must* serve it immediately. By the way, you can fold the omelette over stewed mushrooms, or a spoonful or two of jam, or any other filling you like, and it is just as savoury as when the flavouring is mixed with the eggs."

"Now, Frieda," said Jo, looking questioningly at her.

"Mine is an American recipe," said Frieda. "It is called

SCALLOPED EGGS

Make a mixture of finely chopped ham or bacon, fine breadcrumbs, pepper, salt, and a little melted butter. Moisten with milk into a soft paste. Grease some patty pans, and half fill them with this. Break an egg carefully upon the top of each, dust with pepper and salt, and add a sprinkling of fine white breadcrumbs last. Put into a moderate oven and bake for eight to ten minutes."

"Well, I shall now add our favourite recipe for

SCOTCH EGGS

Hard-boil as many eggs as you require. When done, put them into cold water, and when they are cold, take off the shells, and roll the eggs in flour. Have ready as many sausages as you have eggs; or sausage meat if you prefer it. Wrap the meat round each egg, allowing one fat sausage to an egg. Roll again in flour, coat the eggs with breadcrumbs, and fry in hot fat. When they are done, cut them in two with a sharp knife that has been warmed. They can be served either hot or cold, and garnished with parsley. But be sure you cut a sheet of kitchen paper to fit the dish and set the eggs on that to drain. Otherwise they will be greasy. I have noticed," went on Jo, "that fried things often do look and taste greasy—my own included, so I asked Frau Mieders why last term, and she said it was because so many people won't take the trouble to set fried foods on paper to absorb the fat. I'm passing on the tip here."

"What next?" asked Marie.

"No more egg recipes, anyhow. We'd better be a little careful how much more we add, for I've nearly finished my paper, and as we go home so soon, it isn't worth while sending for more. Besides, it wouldn't get here till after we'd left."

"Well, what else shall we put?"

"How to make good coffee!" said Simone suddenly.

"I'd rather have tea," said Jo. "And anyhow, the last time I had tea in France, it came a lovely pinkish colour! No, Marie; I didn't drink it. I wasn't at all sure what it might be made of, so I abstained. If Simone will give a recipe for coffee, I'll give one for tea—*and* with a few remarks on the subject thrown in. Marie or Frieda can give us one for chocolate, and—"

"Frieda must give us her mother's recipe for lemonade," said Simone decidedly.

"Very well, then; I'll give you chocolate," agreed Marie. "And talking of chocolate, here comes our 'elevenses'. Move that precious book away, Jo, and we'll have it first. I think we ought to try to finish up to-day, anyhow. It looks like clearing up *at last*; and if it does, we must have a good walk to-morrow for our last day. Let's work to-day, and finish. Then Jo can take it home with her, and type it on Dr. Jem's office machine, and then we can send it away. Who knows? By this time next year, we may all be famous!"

"You've got a hope!" said Jo, as she moved her sheets to a side-table. "And you know I can't use the typewriter unless Jem is out. He objects. Has done ever since two or three of the letter-legs—oh, well, the long things the letters are stuck on; *I* don't know what the technical name is!—got stuck together, and when I tried to untangle them I wove them together in some weird way, and the typewriter had to go to Innsbruck to be put right. There was a most colossal row about it, I may say."

DRINKS

DRINKS

"WHAT shall we begin with?" asked Frieda, when they had finished their chocolate and tiny rich cakes.

"Tea, of course!" said Jo promptly. "You always say, '*tea*, coffee, and cocoa'. I'll start off, and the rest of you can follow:

TEA

Tea contains two properties, one called theine, and the other tannin. Theine is the good part; tannin upsets the digestion, though it is very good for burns. There are also two kinds of tea: green and black. Tea is grown in China, India, and Ceylon. I believe they are also experimenting with it in Russia—Georgia, which is in the south. Most people use Indian or Ceylon tea, because it is stronger. In England we add milk; and a good many people take sugar as well. Here and in other countries on the Continent, you have it with slices of lemon; and some folk put in a spoonful of rum. I remember, Frieda," she added, "that the day Grizel and I first came to tea with you, your mother asked us if we wanted lemon or rum with it. I was young and shy then, so goodness knows what would have happened if Bernie hadn't said she knew we preferred milk! And what you idiots are all tittering about in that way, I can't think!" she concluded.

"The idea of you being shy at any time," explained Marie. "I don't believe you ever knew what the word means."

"Oh, don't I? But we haven't time to go into that now. It's not worth while, either. I will continue with my lecture.

"China tea is much paler, and has a much more delicate flavour. In China, it is drunk without milk or sugar, and practically boiling. Here is the way they make it.

"Heat two teapots. Allow one teaspoonful of tea for every two cups. Put the tea into one pot, and pour on it the water which has just come to the boil. Allow the tea to stand for exactly *six* minutes. Then strain it off into the second pot. The idea is to draw out all the theine, and leave the tannin. The longer tea stands, the more tannin you get. That makes the tea bitter, and ruins the flavour. Pour out your two cups, and then rinse the pots for the next two."

"What about Indian and Ceylon tea?" asked Frieda.

"Much more tannin, so never let it stand longer than five minutes before using. By the way, the best tea is made in earthenware teapots. Metal ones spoil the flavour. And if you go camping, you should make billy tea as they do in Australia."

"Billy tea?" The other three stared at her. She explained.

"A billy is just a billy-can—like a smallish dixie, and you know what a dixie is."

"How do you make it?" asked Marie practically.

"I'll tell you. Here goes:

BILLY TEA

Make your fire of wood—in Australia, they generally use the wood of the eucalyptus tree—and set your billy-can full of water on it. As soon as the water comes to the boil, throw in your tea, and remove it from the fire *at once*. Now take a stick, and stir the tea. Wait five minutes, and then pour it off the leaves. The stirring causes all the leaves to go to the bottom, and it has a flavour all its own. Now that is all I can tell you about tea, and it's someone else's turn. Simone, what about your coffee?"

"I hope you do not expect a lecture on coffee," said Simone in some dismay. "I cannot talk as much as you can, Jo, and though I can make coffee, I certainly do not know much about it, nor what its constituents are, except that the main one is caffeine. I can name three or four of the best coffees for you: Royal Java, Blue Mountain, and Mocha. The coffees of Jamaica and Costa Rica are also very good, as is the coffee which comes from Brazil and Kenya."

"Which is the best?" demanded Jo.

"We generally use Mocha, and I know they prefer Royal Java in Holland, but I have heard that Blue Mountain is also very fine."

"Well, that will do for the preliminary remarks," said Jo kindly. "Now get on with the recipe for making REALLY GOOD COFFEE."

"I think," said Simone slowly, "that the real secret of good coffee lies in using it only when freshly roasted and ground. It is better to use a coffee mill, and grind it as you want it. But if you have not one, then keep your coffee in air-tight tins. *Never* leave it in a packet or an open tin. To make it, heat an earthenware jug, and keep it hot. Put in two heaped tablespoonfuls of coffee for a pint of water; the water should be boiling. If you want white coffee, use half a pint of water, and half a pint of milk made *hot* but never *boiling*. After the coffee is made, pour in three—no more—drops of cold water, and stir thoroughly with a large wooden spoon. Then let it stand for five minutes. Pour it through a fine gauze strainer. There is no need to have a percolator if you do this. If you want black coffee, make it a little stronger, and add a pinch of dry mustard to bring out the flavour."

"What about mixing chicory with the coffee?" asked Jo.

"Some people do it, I know. If you ask for coffee in a country farm-house in France, the chances are that what they give you will be mainly chicory. But it gives a bitter taste, and can ruin even good berries. Maman never uses it at all."

"Iced coffee?" queried Marie.

"White coffee, set on ice, with fresh whipped cream floated on top of each cup. I believe they sometimes use ice-cream instead of cream."

"And now, Marie, for chocolate!"

Marie laughed. "You may *say* you prefer tea, Joey; but you do love our chocolate! Here is Mamma's recipe."

CHOCOLATE

To every cup of milk, use one teaspoonful of finely grated chocolate mixed with sugar to taste. Mix this to a paste with cold milk, and when it is quite smooth, pour on boiling milk. Return to the saucepan, and bring again to the boil. Pour it into a jug, and whip with a fork or an egg-whisk till it is frothy, then pour out, and float a spoonful of whipped cream on each cup. You can make cocoa in the same way, and it tastes almost as good as chocolate. If Mamma wants to make the chocolate or cocoa very rich, she uses a little more of each to a given quantity of milk."

"Well, now we know. Now, Frieda, for your lemon syrup, or rather, your mother's. It's one of the nicest drinks I know when you are hot and sticky; it's so cool and refreshing!"

Frieda laughed. "Here is the recipe, then:

LEMON SYRUP

> ONE QUART OF WATER
> THREE CUPS OF SUGAR
> ONE TABLESPOONFUL OF GRATED LEMON RIND
> THREE-QUARTER CUPFUL OF LEMON JUICE
> PINCH OF CITRIC ACID

Boil the sugar and water until you have a thick syrup. Add the lemon juice and rind, or, if you have no lemons, you can use one teaspoonful of good lemon essence. Leave this to get cold. Stir in the acid. Bottle the syrup, and use in the proportion of one tablespoonful to a glass of water."

"And very good it is!" said Jo. "Anyone got anything to add?"

"Yes; Mint Julep!" cried Marie. "I got Corney Flower to give me the recipe, and I remember it, so you can have it."

"Oh, good! Yes; we really oughtn't to miss that one," agreed Jo.

MINT JULEP

FRESH MINT
LEMON JUICE
SUGAR TO TASTE
GINGER ALE

Put a large bunch of freshly cut mint leaves into a jug, and pour over them a cupful of fresh lemon juice. Add four tablespoonfuls of sugar—more if you want it sweet; less if you don't. Strain this, and add to it six bottles of ginger ale. If you have a refrigerator, set it in there for an hour or two, but in any case serve as cold as possible."

"And that finishes the drinks," put in Simone.

Jo nibbled the end of her pen, and stared into space for a moment. "No; not quite. I've just remembered our old recipe for Raspberry Wine. It's very good, and quite easy. Shall we top off with that?"

"Oh, rather! To end with a wine would be so—so elegant!" agreed Marie enthusiastically.

The rest agreed wholeheartedly, so Jo once more set to work:

RASPBERRY WINE

TWO CUPFULS OF SUGAR

THREE CUPFULS OF BOILING WATER
ONE CUPFUL OF FRESH RASPBERRIES
ONE BUNCH OF MINT
TWO CUPFULS OF LIME JUICE

Dissolve the sugar in water, and let it get quite cold. Crush the raspberries and mint together, and add. Pour in the lime juice, and let it stand in the coldest place possible for two to three hours. Then strain, and pour over cracked ice into small glasses. Float a fresh raspberry on each glass, or a few mint leaves if you prefer, and serve.

"This," added Jo, "is *not* one of those things you can bottle. I believe you have to use yeast or alcohol of some sort for that. But it makes a real fancy drink for a big 'do'."

"Well, it is a jolly good wind-up to this part of our book," said Marie. "This afternoon, we must go over the whole MS., and see if there is anything we ought to add. Then we can put it away, and if it is fine to-morrow, we can have a day out for a final treat. Here comes Frau Winkelstein, and I'm ready for Mittagessen, whatever the rest of you may be!"

ODDS AND ENDS

ODDS AND ENDS

THE girls read aloud all that had been written once Mittagessen was cleared away, and a good deal of fun they had over it. Jo flatly refused to do any of the reading.

"No fear!" she said. "I've done all the writing."

"That's just why," murmured Marie gently.

Jo was on her like a flash. "Anything to say about my writing?"

"We-ell, you can't say it's exactly clear," retorted Marie. "However, we're all more or less used to it, so I expect we shall manage to read it somehow. Very well! We'll take it in turns, and you can get on with that little coat you're supposed to be knitting for Sybil. I'm glad I'm not your niece, Joey. If I had to depend on you for woollies, I shouldn't be very warm." And she smiled impishly.

Jo went pink. She had been knitting that same little coat for her small niece, Sybil, all the summer, and it was still far from finished. However, she picked it up, began to knit, and listened carefully to the fruits of their united labour.

When Simone read the last word, Jo looked round on them all. "Do you know, I don't think it's half bad. Well, have we anything to add? I've got two sheets left, and we might as well use them up. What do you suggest, any of you?"

"I should like to say something about the kind of POTS AND PANS that are best for kitchen use," said Frieda.

"We use a good deal of copper in France," said Simone.

"Lovely to look at," agreed Jo, putting down her knitting thankfully, "but an awful bother to keep bright. Give me something that doesn't need polishing, like aluminium, or fireproof ware or glass."

"We, too, use copper," said Frieda. "But many of our saucepans are iron."

"But doesn't that make them very heavy?" asked Simone.

"Well, it does," acknowledged Frieda. "But we have always used them."

"That's one reason why I like aluminium," said Jo, industriously drawing skeletons on her blotting-paper. "And I like glass because you can bring it to table."

"Also, you can see how your cooking is progressing," chimed in Marie.

"Well, I've put down all those suggestions. What should we say next?"

"I think we ought to speak about the LAYING OF THE TABLE," said Marie. "You know yourself, Jo, how much better a meal tastes if the table is prettily laid with sparkling glass and shining silver."

"And flowers," nodded Jo, scribbling hard. "Even if you can't get flowers, you can generally have a vase of leaves. Autumn leaves and berries make lovely table decorations. And so do holly and mistletoe at Christmas. And if you plant bulbs—hyacinths or daffs—they go on for quite a long time. I'd rather have dry bread and tea, and flowers on the table than the richest meal and a table that looks as if someone had just shoved everything on it in a desperate hurry."

The other three agreed with her. Suddenly, Marie began to giggle.

"What is the joke?" asked Simone.

"I was just thinking of a story I've often heard Mamma tell. A friend of hers, who had never done anything in her life, married a poor man. He had a great name, of course, or it wouldn't have been allowed. But he couldn't give the poor girl dozens of well-trained servants. When they had been wedded about five months, Papa and Mamma, who were also newly married, were invited to dinner. Mamma said she never saw such a table. Instead of the knives and forks being laid in the right order, with soup spoons first, on the outside, then fish knives and forks and so on, they were just anyhow. The soup spoons were somewhere in the middle; and the fish things were inside all the rest. The table-napkins were laid across the top of everything, and the glasses arranged in a semicircle above that. But the funniest thing of all"—here Marie lay back in her chair in peals of laughter.

"You stop being so selfish and share the joke with us," wound up Jo. "*What* was the funniest thing?"

"Well, she had given them roast chicken. The husband carved it, and when he plunged his knife into it to begin, the most *awful* smell arose. My dears, what do you think?" Marie looked round on them solemnly. "*She had cooked that chicken with all its insides in!*"

They frankly shouted at this tale of woe. When they were grave again, Marie went on: "Mamma says that was the moment when she vowed to herself that, if she had any daughters, she would see to it that they knew how to do everything about a house, so that they should never make such dreadful mistakes. That's why Wanda and I have learned all sorts of housework, even to cleaning the stoves, and blacking the boots. And Papa decided that his boys should also learn handiwork in the house, for the man was as helpless as the girl. It was a very good thing for them both that two or three years later a rich old great-aunt in America died and left all she had to her nephew, so that they went to New Orleans to live, and were able to have servants to do everything."

"It certainly was," said Frieda. "As for me, both Bernhilda and I have been trained as Mamma was trained. I often wondered about you, Marie. Your father is a Herr Graf, and I always thought girls like you were not taught much in the way of housekeeping."

"In Mamma's time they weren't," said Marie. "But Grandmamma was a very advanced woman, and had Mamma and her sisters all taught how to do things. I think it is a most sensible idea. If ever I have daughters they shall be taught as we were."

"Well, all this is very interesting, but hasn't much to do with our book. Shall we go on? What about weights and measures. Supposing you were stranded on a desert island and you had a few cups and spoons, but no scales or weights, what would you do if your recipes gave pounds and ounces?"

"But there is a measuring table for that," said Simone quickly. "Don't you know it, Joey?" And she solemnly chanted:

> ONE BREAKFASTCUPFUL OF SUGAR EQUALS HALF LB.
> ONE LEVEL TABLESPOONFUL EQUALS ONE OZ.
> ONE BREAKFASTCUPFUL OF FLOUR EQUALS SIX OZ.
> ONE HEAPED TABLESPOONFUL OF FLOUR EQUALS ONE OZ.
> ONE BREAKFASTCUPFUL OF LIQUID EQUALS HALF PINT

"I'll put that down. Say it again, Simone, and slowly, please."

Simone obliged, and then added: "And here is something more. If, when you are making cake, you put a teaspoonful of glycerine into your mixture, the cake will keep fresh for weeks."

"I should like a LIST OF HERBS which are used in the kitchen," said Frieda.

"Oh, yes!" Simone, the girl from the land where herbs are extensively used, fully agreed with this.

So they put their heads together, and finally evolved a list of the better-known herbs and spices. Then Jo wrote it down:

Allspice. The berry of a small tree that grows in the West Indies. It is dried and ground up, and has a flavour of cloves, cinnamon, and nutmeg, and is *not* a mixture of the three.

Angelica. A plant that grows in most parts of the temperate zones of the world. The stalks and leaves are candied, and give an unusual flavour to junkets, custards, and creams. It can also be used for cake and trifle decorations.

Basil, sweet. The leaves have a slight flavour of sweetened cloves. Both leaves and flowers can be used in salads, with turtle soup, and in cooking calves' liver.

Bay leaves can be used fresh or dried. Good for soups and casseroles. And (Jo's contribution, this) two or three bay leaves can be used instead of peach leaves for flavouring custards.

Chervil. Looks and tastes like parsley, and can be used instead of it.

Chives. The leaves are like onion leaves, but have a more delicate flavour.

Cloves. These are the dried buds of the clove tree. Used for flavouring fruits and sauces. Sometimes, when pounded, added to rich fruit cakes.

Dill seeds. These can be used in pickles, and cooked with fish, or put into salads. The leaves can also be used.

Fennel. Has an aniseed flavour, and can be used fresh in salads or as a garnish for fish. The seeds are used in pickles.

Garlic. Has a strong onion flavour, and should be used very sparingly. The best method is to wipe round the dish in which you are going to cook with a garlic clove. The same method will impart the flavour to salad.

Horse radish. The young leaves are used in salads, and the root forms the basis of horse-radish sauce.

Marjoram. The leaves, fresh or dried, are used in various made dishes, soups, and stews. It is sometimes called "Pot Marigold".

Mint. This is used for mint sauce with Lamb. Chopped finely, a little added to a salad is a great improvement.

Parsley. This can be used fresh or fried in most savoury foods.

Pepper. Black pepper is from the ground whole peppercorn, which is the dried berry of the pepper plant. White pepper is from the inner part of the seed, the black, outside coat being removed.

Rue. The blue-green leaves are used fresh or dried in salads and with vegetables.

Sage. This is used for stuffing for goose, duck, and to make a savoury dish with breadcrumbs and suet for pork.

Savoury is used for seasoning and flavouring.

Tansy. The young sprays and leaves are used as flavourings for cakes and puddings. Tansy cakes are traditional in certain English counties at Easter time.

Tarragon. A hot, pungent herb which is used to flavour salads, vinegars, meat, and fish.

Thyme. A sweet, aromatic herb used in stuffings, forcemeats, and savoury meat and fish dishes.

Truffle. A kind of fungus grown underground, which is about the size of a small plum. It is delicious for seasoning and garnishing meats, especially for forcemeat.

"And that's the lot!" said Jo, capping her pen with a sigh of relief. "Oh, I know there are dozens of others; but we've given them enough to go on with, I think. Now, have we really finished? Then—"

A cry from Frieda cut her short. "We have given no invalid dishes! I think we should give one or two at least."

"Quite right," said Jo. "I'll give you Beef Tea for a start."

"And I will give you Chicken Soup," said Simone.

"Then I will give a cooling drink for invalids," said Frieda. "Marie, what about you?"

"I will give you egg coffee, which is very nourishing, and pleasant too."

So once more they set to work. Jo led off with her

BEEF TEA

ONE LB. OF LEAN GRAVY BEEF
ONE AND A HALF CUPS OF WATER
PEPPER AND SALT TO TASTE

Cut up the meat in smallish pieces, and put into a jar or casserole; be sure there is no fat on it. Add the water and salt. Cover the vessel tightly, and put into a very slow oven, and cook very slowly for 2½ to 3 hours. Above all, never let it boil. The meat should be stewed to rags, and when it is cold, it should make a jelly.

"And jolly good it is too!" finished Jo. "Now, your CHICKEN SOUP, Simone."

Simone nodded. "A boiling fowl is required for this; or if you have the bones of a cooked chicken, you can use that. Chop an onion finely, and add a quart of water to each pound of chicken or bones. Then add the onion, and let these ingredients come very slowly to the boil, and simmer gently for two or three hours, removing any scum. Strain, and allow to grow cold. When it is quite cold, remove all the fat. Reheat with a little rice or vermicelli, and serve hot. And," added Simone, "it is quite as good if it is made with rabbit as a substitute. If invalids prefer, it can be left as jelly like Jo's beef tea, and a teaspoonful at a time given."

"Well, here is my cool drink," said Frieda. "Bake about half a dozen tart apples, put them into a quart-sized jug, and cover with boiling water. Leave this to grow cold. Then strain, and sweeten to taste. It is so refreshing. Mamma always makes it for us when we are ill."

"Now for my

EGG COFFEE

Beat one egg in a large cup, adding one-third of a cupful of hot milk. Fill up the cup with hot coffee, and sweeten to taste. The egg, you see, is nourishing," wound up Marie, "and so is the milk. Some people don't like egg and milk, but will take it if it has the coffee flavour. So it is quite good."

"Well, is *that* all?" demanded Jo.

"Oh, I could give you a good many other recipes," returned Simone, "but let us see if we can get this book published. Then, if it sells well, perhaps we could write another."

Jo wrote "Finis" in her largest hand, and surrounded the word with a collection of scrawls supposed to be decorative.

"That's that!" she said, getting up and going to look out of the window. "And now, the sun has actually come out. The roads are swimming with water, of course, but we've all got wellingtons and macs. Let's have Kaffee und Kuchen, and go for a walk. What do you say?"

And with one accord, they all said, "YES!"

COOKING THE BOOK

Thanks are due to Tim and Peter Jolly, who shopped for ingredients, encouraged, stirred (in more senses than one), ate the products, gave honest opinions—and were prepared to take the risk.

There has been much discussion over the years about the recipes in *The Chalet Girls' Cook Book*, and it seems to have been the fashion to assume that none of them would work. Research among our personal friends revealed only that one of them had "once tried the cheese straws, and they turned out all right". We (Adrianne and Ruth) decided to test a wider selection, keeping as open a mind as possible.

The project involved a great deal of running round to each other's house to photograph and taste the products of the experiment. Adrianne owed the Jolly household a dinner, so she got to do the most comprehensive menu, but apart from the Scotch Broth, which was eaten only by the Jollys, we both sampled everything. Isn't it just as well we live near each other!

Scotch Broth—Accent on the 'Scotch'! Why, Ruth wondered, the emphasis on the Scotch, since it doesn't contain any! In the end she concluded that it was a reference to the habits of economy generally attributed to that ancient people. It certainly is a good, basic recipe. Her mother used to make it back in the 1950s when every penny counted. She would have simmered it on the side of the Esse—an Aga by any other name.

"Two lb. of neck of mutton, and any other mutton bones." Ruth remembered her mother buying "neck of lamb", which she also called "stewing lamb" or "scrag end". Local butchers used to supply this, but she hadn't seen it of recent years. None of the supermarkets stocked it, so she and her husband Tim went on an expedition to the only butcher's left in town. She hoped they would know what she meant when she said "good old-fashioned stewing lamb, please!"

"Ah, you want scrag," said the butcher.

"Exactly," Ruth beamed.

They waited while he cut it up. He didn't have any ready prepared either.

Tim bought a pack of mixed vegetables from the supermarket. It contained four smallish carrots, one swede, one onion and one leek. No celery, but otherwise a pretty good match.

"One large cup of barley; one large cup of lentils—*soaked overnight, or they won't soften*." Ruth wasn't sure what a "large cup" was to Joey, so she used the cup marker on her cook's measure. (This seemed, as it turned out, to be probably a bit more than was intended.) She had managed to remember to put the lentils to soak.

"Pepper and salt to taste." Yes, she had those, though she normally uses almost no salt. This needed some, though.

"Put your bones and meat into a pan with two quarts of water; add the barley and lentils, and let them boil with the lid on till nearly cooked."

Ruth couldn't get the full two quarts into the pan at first, so added the last pint gradually during the course of the cooking. Not knowing how long it would take for them to be "nearly cooked", she decided to check after half an hour. In the end she boiled them for about 40 minutes, by which time the barley was cooked but not fully softened, and the meat was done but not to the point of dropping off the bone.

At this point Ruth realised that she couldn't possibly stay up another two hours, so she decided to resume the procedure next evening when they would actually be eating it. She wouldn't recommend a 24-hour break in this recipe: pearl barley, it would appear, will continue to swell as long as there is anything for it to absorb. By next day she had a pan full of something resembling porridge, with large lumps of lamb at intervals. She added the final half pint of water and hoped for the best.

"Cut up the vegetables into small cubes, and pop them in with the pepper and salt, and simmer for two hours."

Tim nobly reheated the "porridge" while Ruth peeled and chopped the vegetables. They'd both had long days at work and it was late, so Ruth was secretly hoping to cut the cooking time to a more reasonable 20 minutes or so. With that in mind, she pre-softened the onion in a frying pan, because she really hates undercooked onion.

Although she was using an eight-pint casserole, it was very full by now, so she took the meat out while she cooked the veg. Joey doesn't mention whether to take the meat off the bone or leave it on. Ruth decided it would be too much hassle to debone it, so left it on. Joey doesn't mention removing the "any other mutton bones" either, leaving one with a pleasing picture of her dishing up a nice plateful of bones!

The trouble with trying to cook cubes of vegetables in porridge is that the porridge erupts and constantly

Scotch Broth

flings them to the surface, so it's hard to keep them hot enough for them to cook. She didn't dare put the lid on (as Joey instructs), because the glutinous mass she had created would undoubtedly have stuck to the bottom of the pan. So Tim virtuously stood and stirred the thing till the veg was done. He says he stirred it for an hour. Ruth maintains that this claim was just stirring! But it was certainly over half an hour.

"By the way, if you let it boil, it comes queer and thin, so don't!"

They let it boil. They let it boil and boil. They would have loved it to "come queer and thin" instead of throwing up bubbles like Vesuvius. Thin it was not, even though Ruth sneakily added quite a lot more water.

"Sprinkle on a little chopped parsley just before serving."

Ruth culled some parsley from the pot on the window-sill and got out the herb chopper. That bit worked perfectly.

"Grand for a cold day!"

The verdict from the family? "Excellent!" and "This meat is delicious!"

Another time Ruth would follow the advice in her *Good Housekeeping* book and add the barley later, at the same time as the vegetables. She'd probably pressure-cook the meat and bones, too. And she certainly wouldn't take a break from cooking after the barley was in. But it worked!

She'd say it served 4–6 as a main course.

Now it was Adrianne's turn. Originally it was supposed to be a normal Sunday lunch, as a thank you to Tim for wiring in the new cooker for her—and a chance to put it through its paces. She thought she might possibly try a dessert from the *Cook Book* as part of her experiment for this article, but the whole meal turned out to be a *Cook Book* menu, from start to finish. However, she did not mention that to the visiting menfolk—at least, not prior to the fact!

Adrianne started the day making Marie's **Sand Cake** to go with the after-lunch drinks. It needed a slow oven, so she wanted it done well before she needed to be cooking the main meal. She duly followed the instructions, but read the recipe twice to assure herself that it really did say *roll* the pieces out: the consistency was much more runny cake than dough. Even with extra flour on the board, the mixture would simply have oozed its way to the floor. What had she done wrong? She'd followed the recipe! The only thing she can think is that the eggs may have been larger than EBD anticipated—Adrianne used large eggs (free range, of course), so perhaps three small eggs or even just two large eggs would have been sufficient. So she added more flour … and more flour … and … Yes, she ended up doubling the flour quantity. If she'd been used to working with almonds, she would perhaps have thought to add more of those as well, but she didn't, so … but more of that later.

Adrianne now had a dough-like mix, but rather than roll it, she confesses she simply cut the lump in three (well, actually six: because she doesn't own a large cake tin, she used two small loaf tins), and

Sand Cake in the making

pressed the first layer into the base of the tin. The recipe called for "marmalade or some other preserve"; Adrianne used strawberry conserve, since she's a red jam person. Two cakes were soon layered in their tins and popped into the oven.

"When it is half-baked, pour over it a water icing, return to the oven, and finish baking."

Having never made—or even seen—Sand Cake before, Adrianne wasn't at all sure what constituted "half-baked"! She checked it after 15 minutes but the top still seemed quite soft, so she left it for another 10 minutes. By this time the top was beginning to crunch up a little, so she guessed that would do. The

Well, that looks interesting!

icing went on easily enough, and she put the cakes back in the oven for another 20 minutes or so.

Now came the tricky part. What she hadn't allowed for was the fact that this cake was in *layers*. As she had spread the jam right to the edges, the cake *stayed* in layers—*separate* layers! So when the cakes were turned out, she had layers sliding all over the place and hot jam dripping on to the tray she had—with great foresight—placed beneath the cooling rack. What she *should* have done was to keep a border of cake dough so that the layers could seal themselves, thus baking as a solid cake—and keeping the jam inside.

While the cake was cooling, Adrianne got on with the **Blackberry Fluff**. As she read through Simone's recipe with a sinking feeling, she thought, "Should have done this last night!" Would it set in time? She checked cupboards and assured herself that she had all the necessary ingredients for apple crumble, just in case she had to come up with something else in a hurry …

She set the blackberries cooking and looked at the directions on the gelatine box. The *Cook Book* said to use a dessertspoonful of gelatine powder. The box said one sachet (equivalent of her dessertspoon) would be suitable for 1 litre of liquid. Looking at the blackberry concoction in the pan, Adrianne was fairly sure it was more than a litre, so she measured it: sure enough, it was about 1½ litres, so she used 1½ sachets, and set the pan by the open window to cool—it was several degrees cooler outside than in on this chilly autumn day. Once it was cool enough to move to the fridge, she transferred it, but she had her doubts: it still slopped around the pan in a very free and easy manner! Still, no time to think about that. She had a main meal to put together.

Pulling out all the vegetables, Adrianne realised she had a lot of potatoes—more than she could eat on her own before they went off—so she thought she'd try making Marie's **Potato Soup** as a starter. She doesn't have onion in the house, so she had to skip that part of the recipe. She quickly peeled the potatoes and set them to boil. When they were ready, she drained off the water, added the milk and set it all to simmering. "Till the potatoes have gone," says Marie. Gone? Gone where? Adrianne had finished all the other preparations for lunch, the guests had arrived, and the potatoes were still soft cubes simmering happily in the milk! So out came the trusty potato masher, and after a few more minutes on the hob, we had soup. It must have been all right, as everyone had seconds.

Meanwhile, the main course was cooking itself. Simone suggested salting the inside of the **Roast Chicken** and trussing it. Since at least one person at the meal table was on a salt-restricted diet—and Adrianne in any case has hardly used salt in years—she skipped that part; and the bird came ready trussed, so she didn't need to do anything about that. Simone also suggested cooking in a little salted water; Adrianne opted for a little vegetable oil and honey instead. Where Simone cooked her chicken in a casserole, crisping the skin at the end of the cooking time, Adrianne did hers on a roasting tray, starting the cooking on high for the

Mashing the soup

first 15 minutes and then reducing the temperature. She still achieved the brown and crispy skin, but she did it in the opposite order. As suggested by Marie, the **Roast Vegetables** were all much the same size, and as many as could fit went into the roasting tray with the chicken. The rest went on to a second tray with a light coating of vegetable oil. Halfway through the cooking, Adrianne transferred a little of the honeyed oil from the roasting pan to the vegetable tray so that all the vegetables would take on some of the flavour. Along with the fresh green beans, the roast chicken and vegetables—potato, squash and sweet potato—were a definite winner.

Sure there's enough?

Potato Soup, Roast Chicken, Blackberry Fluff, and Sand Cake

Now for that Fluff. When Adrianne had checked its cooling progress earlier, she hadn't been convinced that it was setting, but nevertheless she added the beaten egg whites: it would work or it wouldn't, but if it was going to have any chance of doing so, she needed to finish the preparations. She poured the mixture into individual glass bowls: again, hoping to give it every chance of setting in time. An hour later there were definite signs of thickening, and by the time the guests arrived, the desserts had set—a great surprise, considering she'd only started the process some three-and-a-half hours earlier! She whipped up some cream to decorate the Fluff, and we all cleared our bowls: this particular recipe was declared a howling success.

But would the Sand Cake survive the taste test? Admittedly, we'd done ourselves proud on the previous courses, so we didn't really have any room for cake. The men looked at the offering on their plates, and very clearly they were wondering if they could get away with pleading overindulgence, but bravely we all ploughed on! The final product was satisfactory if a little heavy. As already noted, Adrianne had added extra flour to gain the right consistency for rolling, and Ruth suggested adding extra ground almonds as well might have retained the cake's moistness. So not a huge success, but still quite edible.

Who would have thought one might provide a three-course meal, plus cake, from the *Cook Book*, and the guests still be willing to come back another time?

But our experiment was not yet finished.

The next day Ruth bagged the **Kedgeree** as a soft option, since it's pretty much the way she makes kedgeree anyway, though she uses tinned kippers rather than salmon.

"One hard-boiled egg cut into slices"—we used three eggs as we were doubling the quantities and we wanted some yolk for decoration, as Joey suggests.

"Half lb. of cold cooked fish or a tin of salmon"—we used the salmon, so we could test out the vaunted prettiness of this dish.

"Melt the fat in a pan, and add the rice, the egg, and the fish." First cook your rice! Secure in the knowledge that she could have used Joey's Indian method, Ruth saved time and effort and put it in the rice cooker as usual. She also chopped the eggs rather than slice them, as this seemed more practical when they were going to be stirred into rice. "Season with salt and pepper. For 'them as likes it' you can add a touch of curry, but it should be only a touch. Curry

Kedgeree

powder is on the powerful side." We didn't add any salt as the salmon was already salty. We did put in a little garam masala, but it didn't really affect the taste—maybe we should have used a more powerful curry powder. We found that the rice tended to stick to the pan in spite of the melted butter, so we pre-warmed the salmon in a separate pan to reduce the re-heating time. "When the kedgeree is hot, pile it on a warm dish, and decorate it with sprays of parsley and some of the yolk of the egg, which you should keep for the purpose. You must sieve that, so that it makes a golden powder over the white of the rice." Sieving the egg yolk didn't seem like an option, as the eggs were not boiled quite hard enough. We crumbled it instead. "The green and white and gold—and pink, if you use salmon—really makes this a very pretty dish." Tasty, too—and very easy.

Adrianne volunteered to make the **Venetian Ladies**—very noble of her since she doesn't eat tomatoes herself! Tim was out, so she only made two rather than the four suggested in the recipe. Our local supermarket didn't carry shallots, so she replaced this ingredient with the bulbs of some spring onions.

Marie instructs: "Cut the tomatoes in half, and scoop out the pulp." It seemed a pity to waste the pulp, so Ruth ate it while Adrianne made faces. "Fill the tomato case with the peas or beans, shallot, rasher, and seasoning which you will have previously mixed together." We used beans as our green vegetable. Not only had we previously mixed the ingredients together; we had lightly cooked the bacon and onion, as we weren't sure that ten minutes in the oven would suffice for these. "Put them into a buttered baking dish, and cover thickly with grated cheese. Bake for ten minutes. Serve on slices of fried bread cut into rounds." We omitted the fried bread as we were using these as a side dish for a main meal. Adrianne just had beans for hers.

The Ladies getting dressed for dinner

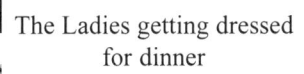

Apple Charlotte ready for the oven

"'Isn't it rather finicky to make?' asked Jo." As tomatoes go, this *was* quite finicky, but it made a very interesting vegetable, and we felt Marie would have approved, as the dark green beans and pink bacon bits looked very pretty in the tomato cases. Ruth would probably make this again. Adrianne would make it to serve to visitors but not for herself!

We finished off that particular meal with Jo's **Apple Charlotte**. "Thickly grease your piedish with butter or marge, and sprinkle this with sugar—brown is best if you have it handy. You can also use honey or golden syrup." Ruth always has brown sugar handy, as she much prefers it, so we used that.

"Now put in a layer of soft white breadcrumbs; then a layer of stewed apple; then more breadcrumbs, and so on, until the dish is full." This recipe rather starts off in the middle and assumes a ready supply of stewed apple. Before sending Peter to the supermarket, Ruth had consulted her Cordon Bleu cook book for additional guidance and discovered that she needed 1½ lbs of cooking apples and 2 oz white breadcrumbs. The recipe also recommended 3 oz sugar—again we used brown—and the grated rind of half a lemon, but we hadn't got one so we just shook in some lemon juice.

In fact we used at least 3 oz of breadcrumbs. The Cordon Bleu book wanted us to mix them with sugar, but Joey only mentions sugar with the bottom and top layers so that's how we did it.

"Finish off with a layer of breadcrumbs and sugar. Put a few dabs of your fat over all, and bake golden-brown in a moderate oven." The Cordon Bleu book said "for 40–50 minutes", which was a useful indication when it came to timing the meal. The Apple Charlotte had to share the oven with some Schnitzel-like breaded chicken pieces (OK, they weren't home made!) and the Venetian Ladies, so it was at a high temperature for part of the time, but we put it on the bottom shelf and it didn't seem to mind. It was a mouth-watering success.

We served it with **Custard**—Joey's recipe: there's just so much enterprising hard work one can manage after a long day in the office!

We realised we hadn't done anything from the cheese section. We already knew the cheese straws were good, and weren't looking for any more fattening snacks after having dessert twice in one week already. So we decided to aim for a main meal, and chose the **Cheese Casserole**. Simone says: "Cook some carrots, parsnips, turnips, potatoes, an onion, celery, or any other root vegetable you can find. Cold cauliflower is also good in this. Cut up your selection into small cubes." Ruth looked in her fridge and came up with two enormous carrots, which she duly cut into cubes. There was most of a pack of mixed cauliflower and broccoli florets, so we added those to the pan, plus the beans left over from the Venetian Ladies, cut into one-inch lengths. All these needed about the same time to cook, which was very convenient. We put them on to boil, and started to make the cheese sauce.

It's generally accepted in the Jolly household that Adrianne makes the world's best cheese sauce, smooth and delicious, so she was the obvious choice for this part of the recipe. She's an intuitive cook who doesn't do much measuring, but when we thought back afterwards, she had followed Simone's **Cheese Sauce** recipe pretty much exactly, with the quantities doubled. At the last minute we remembered the mustard and cayenne pepper so we sprinkled these on the top and beat them in thoroughly.

"Butter a casserole and sprinkle it over with grated cheese." Ruth had never lined a dish with cheese before, but she obediently did so. "Fill the dish with the diced vegetables, and cover with a thick cheese sauce." As there was quite a lot of parmesan left over from the Venetian Ladies, we also sprinkled this on top of the sauce to help it brown. "Bake in a moderate oven for about quarter of an hour, and see that the top is a warm brown. Serve hot." We did, and it was delicious! We served it with rice, to give it more body and make it less rich.

When we came to review the recipes we'd tried so far, we realised that we'd done nothing from the Egg section of the *Cook Book*, nor had we used any of Frieda's recipes. **Scalloped Eggs** looked quite reasonable, and would make a tasty starter for an evening meal, we decided.

"Make a mixture of finely chopped ham or bacon, fine breadcrumbs, pepper, salt, and a little melted

Cheese Casserole: Before and After

butter." We used one rasher of bacon, which we chopped and lightly fried before mixing it with 2¼ oz of breadcrumbs and a teaspoonful of marge, melted. If we'd read the recipe through in advance we'd have known to reserve a small quantity of breadcrumbs—as it was, Ruth had to produce some more! "Moisten with milk into a soft paste." Ruth reckoned it was not exactly a paste, more like a bread poultice. She said that never in her wildest dreams had she thought of baking an egg on a bread poultice base. But she did it anyway. "Grease some patty pans, and half fill them with this." We used ramekins, and we gave the bread mixture two

Frieda's Scalloped Egg

minutes in the oven before adding the eggs because we felt the ramekins would need to heat through properly, being china rather than metal. "Break an egg carefully upon the top of each, dust with pepper and salt, and add a sprinkling of fine white breadcrumbs last. Put into a moderate oven and bake for eight to ten minutes." We set the fan oven to 160C, about gas mark 4, and gave them eight minutes. The eggs were rather lightly set in the middle so maybe another minute or so wouldn't have hurt. To everyone's amazement, the bread and bacon poultice was delicious with the baked eggs!

And as the finale for this cookery tour de force, we just had to make the **Mint Julep**.

"Put a large bunch of freshly cut mint leaves into a jug, and pour over them a cupful of fresh lemon juice." This sounded like a lot of lemon juice. For a change we tried an ordinary teacup instead of the measuring cup, but it turned out to be almost exactly the same volume. "Add four tablespoonfuls of sugar—more if you want it sweet; less if you don't." Not knowing what to expect, we went with the four. We also stirred it until dissolved, feeling that this instruction could be assumed. "Strain this, and add to it six bottles of ginger ale." Adrianne found out the size of a 1950s bottle of ginger ale from the internet, multiplied by six and came up with 1.25 litres near enough. We had a 1 litre bottle, which we decided would do. "If you have a refrigerator, set it in there for an hour or two, but in any case serve as cold as possible."

Ruth was not convinced that just pouring the lemon juice over the mint leaves and then straining it pretty much immediately was going to produce anything mint flavoured at all. In fact, we both found this recipe rather improbable. Research on the internet told us that mint julep relies on a really good bourbon whisky for success(!), but we persevered and eventually found a non-alcoholic version which was almost identical to Corney's, so we apologised mentally. The difference was that the new recipe required the lemon juice and sugar to stand on the mint leaves for 30 minutes before straining and adding the ginger ale.

We made the mint, lemon and sugar mixture and divided it into two, following Joey's instructions with one portion and treating the other according to the internet recipe. Both tasted minty, but predictably the one which had been left to stand with the leaves in was noticeably mintier. Adrianne preferred Joey's version and Ruth preferred the mintier one. Peter declined to state his preference and went off to brew coffee.

Time for a refreshing drink!

So are the recipes in this book a disaster, as we have occasionally heard it whispered? Well, we've tried a range of dishes, and not always the easiest options, and although we've sometimes had to make adjustments, we have to say that the general verdict was overwhelmingly positive.

Adrianne Fitzpatrick and Ruth Jolly

ERRORS IN THE FIRST EDITION

In republishing *The Chalet Girls' Cook Book* we have kept to the text of the first edition. We have neither edited nor updated it—leaving the reader to determine whether Frau Annich and Frau Winkelstein are one person or two, and whose recipe the cucumber cream actually is—but have corrected obvious typographical errors wherever it was possible to be sure what the author intended. It's not our policy to correct French or German usage, but we did feel justified in changing Innsbrück to Innsbruck and Liebeströume to Liebesträume, as these were obvious slips. We hope we have not allowed any new errors to creep in.

Punctuation
We have added a missing apostrophe and removed two spurious ones; we have also added a missing quotation mark and removed another, and have added a full stop.

Variant usages
We have standardised the following:

    coco-nut, not cocoa-nut
    Blue Mountain [coffee], not Blue mountain

Incorrect words

We found three places where words had been misspelled or used in error, and we have corrected these:

>page 43, paragraph 4, line 1: 'Joe'—'Jo'
>page 77, paragraph 3, line 3: 'curley'—'curly'
>page 146, paragraph 1, line 2: 'Come one!'—'Come on!'

Ruth Jolly and Alison Neale

APPENDIX: RECIPES FROM *THE THIRD CHALET BOOK FOR GIRLS*

Fruit Crunch
3 ozs. flour. 2 ozs. fat. 1 oz. sugar. Fruit.

This is good with any fruit, but I am giving it with apples. Half fill a medium-sized piedish with sliced apple. Add 2 tablespoonfuls of water and a sprinkling of sugar and a pinch of salt. Now rub your fat into the flour till it looks like fine breadcrumbs. Do this with the *tips* of your fingers. Stir in the sugar, and then cover your fruit with it. Put into a moderate oven, and bake until the fruit is soft.

Cookie Biscuits
1 oz. rolled oats. 2 ozs. flour. 1 dessertspoonful golden syrup. ½ oz. sugar. 1 oz. fat. 1 egg or the same quantity of egg-powder. Pinch of salt. Pinch of baking powder.

Mix the flour, oats, sugar, salt, and a *good* pinch of baking powder together. Rub in the fat. Then stir in your golden syrup, and last of all your egg, well beaten till it is all frothy. Stir until it is a stiff dough. Then flour your baking board, and on it roll the dough to a thickness of one-eighth of an inch. Cut out rounds with a cake-cutter or the lid of a cocoa-tin. Bake in a moderate oven for 20 minutes on a well-greased baking-tin. When done, cool on wire tray.

Stovies

Fry 4 ozs. onion in ½ oz. cooking fat. Add 1 lb. of potatoes sliced and seasoned with pepper and salt. Pour in ¾ pint stock or water, cover the pan and cook for 1 hour, stirring occasionally.

Soda Scones

1 lb. plain flour. 1 oz. margarine. ¾ teaspoonful each of salt and bicarbonate of soda. 1 teaspoonful cream of tartar.

Mix flour and salt. Rub in the margarine, and then mix the bicarbonate of soda and cream of tartar together, and add enough buttermilk or fresh milk to make a stiff dough. Roll out on a floured board to a thickness of ½ inch, and cut out into rounds. Bake in a moderate oven until they are golden brown. If you use sour milk, you must use less soda and cream of tartar.

DISCOVERING THE CHALET SCHOOL SERIES

In 1925 W & R Chambers Ltd published *The School at the Chalet*, the first title in Elinor Brent-Dyer's Chalet School series. Forty-five years later, in 1970, the same company published the final title in the series, *Prefects of the Chalet School*. It was published posthumously, EBD (as she is known to her fans) having signed the contract three days before she died. During those 45 years Elinor wrote around 60 Chalet School titles, the School moved from the Austrian Tyrol to Guernsey, England, Wales and finally Switzerland, a fan club flourished, and the books began to appear in an abridged paperback format.

How Many Chalet School Titles Are There?
Numbering the Chalet School titles is not as easy as it might appear. The back of the Chambers dustwrapper of *Prefects of the Chalet School* offers a simple list of titles, numbered 1–58. However, no 31, *Tom Tackles the Chalet School*, was published out of sequence (see below), and there were five 'extra' titles, of which one, *The Chalet School and Rosalie*, follows just after *Tom* in the series chronology. In addition, there was a long 'short' story, *The Mystery at the Chalet School*, which comes just before *Tom*. Helen McClelland, EBD's biographer, helpfully devised the system of re-numbering these titles 19a, 19b and 19c (see list on page 217).

    Further complications apply when looking at the paperbacks. In a number of cases, Armada split the original hardbacks into two when publishing them in paperback, and this meant that the paperbacks are numbered 1–62. In addition, *The Mystery at the Chalet School* was only ever published in paperback with *The Chalet School and Rosalie* but should be numbered 21a in this sequence (see list on page 220).

Girls Gone By are following the numbering system of the original hardbacks. All titles will eventually be republished, but not all will be in print at the same time.

Apart from *The Chalet School and Rosalie*, Chambers published four other 'extra' titles: *The Chalet Book for Girls*, *The Second Chalet Book for Girls*, *The Third Chalet Book for Girls* and *The Chalet Girls' Cook Book*. *The Chalet Book for Girls* included *The Mystery at the Chalet School* as well as three other Chalet School short stories, one non-Chalet story by EBD, and four articles. *The Second Chalet Book for Girls* included the first half of *Tom Tackles the Chalet School*, together with two Chalet School short stories, one other story by EBD, seven articles (including the start of what was to become *The Chalet Girls' Cook Book*) and a rather didactic photographic article called *Beth's Diary*, which featured Beth Chester going to Devon and Cornwall. *The Third Chalet Book for Girls* included the second half of *Tom Tackles the Chalet School* (called *Tom Plays the Game*) as well as two Chalet School short stories, three other stories by EBD and three articles. (Clearly the dustwrapper was printed before the book, since the back flap lists three stories and two articles which are not in the book.) It is likely that *The Chalet School and Rosalie* was intended to be the long story for a fourth *Book for Girls*, but since no more were published this title eventually appeared in 1951 in paperback (very unusual for the time). The back cover of *The Second Chalet Book for Girls* lists *The First Junior Chalet Book* as hopefully being published 'next year'; this never materialised. *The Chalet Girls' Cook Book* is not merely a collection of recipes but also contains a very loose story about Joey, Simone, Marie and Frieda just after they have left the School. While not all of these Chalet stories add crucial information to the series, many of them do, and they are certainly worth collecting. All the *Books for Girls* are difficult to obtain on the second-hand market, but most of the stories were reprinted in two books compiled by Helen McClelland, *Elinor M. Brent-Dyer's Chalet School* (out of print) and *The Chalet School Companion* (available from Bettany Press). Girls Gone By have now published all EBD's known short stories, from these and other sources, in a single volume.

The Locations of the Chalet School Books
The Chalet School started its life in Briesau am Tiernsee in the Austrian Tyrol (Pertisau am Achensee in real life). After Germany signed the Anschluss with Austria in 1938, it would have been impossible to keep even a fictional school in Austria. As a result, EBD wrote *The Chalet School in Exile*, during which, following an encounter with some Nazis, several of the girls, including Joey Bettany, were forced to flee Austria, and the School was also forced to leave. Unfortunately, Elinor chose to move the School to Guernsey—the book was published just as Germany invaded the Channel Islands. The next book, *The Chalet School Goes to It*, saw the School moving again, this time to a village near Armiford—Hereford in real life. Here the School remained for the duration of the war, and indeed when the next move came, in *The Chalet School and the Island*, it was for reasons of plot. The island concerned was off the south-west coast of Wales, and is fictional, although generally agreed by Chalet School fans to be a combination of various islands including Caldey Island, St Margaret's Isle, Skokholm, Ramsey Island and Grassholm, with Caldey Island being the most likely contender if a single island has to be picked. Elinor had long

wanted to move the School back to Austria, but the political situation there in the 1950s forbade such a move, so she did the next best thing and moved it to Switzerland, firstly by establishing a finishing branch in *The Chalet School in the Oberland*, and secondly by relocating the School itself in *The Chalet School and Barbara*. The exact location is subject to much debate, but it seems likely that it is somewhere near Wengen in the Bernese Oberland. Here the School was to remain for the rest of its fictional life, and here it still is today for its many aficionados.

The Chalet Club 1959–69
In 1959 Chambers and Elinor Brent-Dyer started a club for lovers of the Chalet books, beginning with 33 members. When the club closed in 1969, after Elinor's death, there were around 4,000 members worldwide. Twice-yearly News Letters were produced, written by Elinor herself, and the information in these adds fascinating, if sometimes conflicting, detail to the series. In 1997 Friends of the Chalet School, one of the two fan clubs existing today, republished the News Letters in facsimile book format. Girls Gone By Publishers produced a new edition in 2004.

The Publication of the Chalet School Series in Armada Paperback
On 1 May 1967, Armada, the children's paperback division of what was then William Collins, Sons & Co Ltd, published the first four Chalet School paperbacks. This momentous news was covered in issue Number Sixteen of the Chalet Club News Letter, which also appeared in May 1967. In her editorial, Elinor Brent-Dyer said: 'Prepare for a BIG piece of news. The Chalet Books, slightly abridged, are

being reissued in the Armada series. The first four come out in May, and two of them are *The School at the Chalet* and *Jo of the Chalet School*. So watch the windows of the booksellers if you want to add them to your collection. They will be issued at the usual Armada price, which should bring them within the reach of all of you. I hope you like the new jackets. Myself, I think them charming, especially *The School at the Chalet*.' On the back page of the News Letter there was an advertisement for the books, which reproduced the covers of the first four titles.

The words 'slightly abridged' were a huge understatement, and over the years Chalet fans have made frequent complaints about the fact that the paperbacks are abridged, about some of the covers, and about the fact that the books were published in a most extraordinary order, with the whole series never available in paperback at any one time. It has to be said, however, that were it not for the paperbacks interest in the Chalet series would, in the main, be confined to those who had bought or borrowed the hardbacks prior to their demise in the early 1970s, and Chalet fans would mostly be at least 40 and over in age. The paperbacks have sold hundreds of thousands of copies over the years, and those that are not in print (the vast majority) are still to be found on the second-hand market (through charity shops and jumble sales as well as dealers). They may be cut (and sometimes disgracefully so), but enough of the story is there to fascinate new readers, and we should be grateful that they were published at all. Had they not been, it is most unlikely that two Chalet clubs would now be flourishing and that Girls Gone By Publishers would be able to republish the series in this new, unabridged, format.

Clarissa Cridland

ELINOR M BRENT-DYER: A BRIEF BIOGRAPHY

EBD was born Gladys Eleanor May Dyer in South Shields on 6 April 1894, the only daughter of Eleanor (Nelly) Watson Rutherford and Charles Morris Brent Dyer. Her father had been married before and had a son, Charles Arnold, who was never to live with his father and stepmother. This caused some friction between Elinor's parents, and her father left home when she was three and her younger brother, Henzell, was two. Her father eventually went to live with another woman by whom he had a third son, Morris. Elinor's parents lived in a respectable lower-middle-class area, and the family covered up the departure of her father by saying that her mother had 'lost' her husband.

In 1912 Henzell died of cerebro-spinal fever, another event which was covered up. Friends of Elinor's who knew her after his death were unaware that she had had a brother. Death from illness was, of course, common at this time, and Elinor's familiarity with this is reflected in her books, which abound with motherless heroines.

Elinor was educated privately in South Shields, and returned there to teach after she had been to the City of Leeds Training College. In the early 1920s she adopted the name Elinor Mary Brent-Dyer. She was interested in the theatre, and her first book, *Gerry Goes to School*, published in 1922, was written for the child actress Hazel Bainbridge—mother of the actress Kate O'Mara. In the mid 1920s she also taught at St Helen's, Northwood, Middlesex, at Moreton House School, Dunstable, Bedfordshire, and in Fareham near Portsmouth. She was a keen musician and a practising Christian, converting to Roman Catholicism in 1930, a major step in those days.

In the early 1920s Elinor spent a holiday in the Austrian Tyrol at Pertisau am Achensee, which she was to use so successfully as the first location in the Chalet School series. (Many of the locations in her books were real places.) In 1933 she moved with her mother and stepfather to Hereford, travelling daily to Peterchurch as a governess. After her stepfather died in November 1937 she started her own school in Hereford, The Margaret Roper, which ran from 1938 until 1948. Unlike the Chalet School it was not a huge success and probably would not have survived had it not been for the Second World War. From 1948 Elinor devoted all her time to writing. Her mother died in 1957, and in 1964 Elinor moved to Redhill, Surrey, where she died on 20 September 1969.

Clarissa Cridland

COMPLETE NUMERICAL LIST OF TITLES IN THE CHALET SCHOOL SERIES
(Chambers and Girls Gone By)
Dates in parentheses refer to the original publication dates

1. *The School at the Chalet* (1925)
2. *Jo of the Chalet School* (1926)
3. *The Princess of the Chalet School* (1927)
4. *The Head Girl of the Chalet School* (1928)
5. *The Rivals of the Chalet School* (1929)
6. *Eustacia Goes to the Chalet School* (1930)
7. *The Chalet School and Jo* (1931)
8. *The Chalet Girls in Camp* (1932)
9. *The Exploits of the Chalet Girls* (1933)
10. *The Chalet School and the Lintons* (1934) (published in Armada paperback in two volumes—*The Chalet School and the Lintons* and *A Rebel at the Chalet School*)
11. *The New House at the Chalet School* (1935)
12. *Jo Returns to the Chalet School* (1936)
13. *The New Chalet School* (1938) (published in Armada paperback in two volumes—*The New Chalet School* and *A United Chalet School*)
14. *The Chalet School in Exile* (1940)
15. *The Chalet School Goes to It* (1941) (published in Armada paperback as *The Chalet School at War*)
16. *The Highland Twins at the Chalet School* (1942)
17. *Lavender Laughs in the Chalet School* (1943) (published in Armada paperback as *Lavender Leigh at the Chalet School*)
18. *Gay From China at the Chalet School*

(1944) (published in Armada paperback as *Gay Lambert at the Chalet School*)
19. *Jo to the Rescue* (1945)
19a. *The Mystery at the Chalet School* (1947) (published in *The Chalet Book for Girls*)
19b. *Tom Tackles the Chalet School* (published in *The Second Chalet Book for Girls*, 1948, and *The Third Chalet Book for Girls*, 1949, and then as a single volume in 1955)
19c. *The Chalet School and Rosalie* (1951) (published as a paperback)
20. *Three Go to the Chalet School* (1949)
21. *The Chalet School and the Island* (1950)
22. *Peggy of the Chalet School* (1950)
23. *Carola Storms the Chalet School* (1951)
24. *The Wrong Chalet School* (1952)
25. *Shocks for the Chalet School* (1952)
26. *The Chalet School in the Oberland* (1952)
27. *Bride Leads the Chalet School* (1953)
28. *Changes for the Chalet School* (1953)
29. *Joey Goes to the Oberland* (1954)
30. *The Chalet School and Barbara* (1954)
31. (see 19b)
32. *The Chalet School Does It Again* (1955)
33. *A Chalet Girl from Kenya* (1955)
34. *Mary-Lou of the Chalet School* (1956)
35. *A Genius at the Chalet School* (1956) (published in Armada paperback in two volumes—*A Genius at the Chalet School* and *Chalet School Fête*)
36. *A Problem for the Chalet School* (1956)
37. *The New Mistress at the Chalet School* (1957)
38. *Excitements at the Chalet School* (1957)
39. *The Coming of Age of the Chalet School* (1958)
40. *The Chalet School and Richenda* (1958)
41. *Trials for the Chalet School* (1958)
42. *Theodora and the Chalet School* (1959)

43. *Joey and Co. in Tirol* (1960)
44. *Ruey Richardson—Chaletian* (1960) (published in Armada paperback as *Ruey Richardson at the Chalet School*)
45. *A Leader in the Chalet School* (1961)
46. *The Chalet School Wins the Trick* (1961)
47. *A Future Chalet School Girl* (1962)
48. *The Feud in the Chalet School* (1962)
49. *The Chalet School Triplets* (1963)
50. *The Chalet School Reunion* (1963)
51. *Jane and the Chalet School* (1964)
52. *Redheads at the Chalet School* (1964)
53. *Adrienne and the Chalet School* (1965)
54. *Summer Term at the Chalet School* (1965)
55. *Challenge for the Chalet School* (1966)
56. *Two Sams at the Chalet School* (1967)
57. *Althea Joins the Chalet School* (1969)
58. *Prefects of the Chalet School* (1970)

Extras

The Chalet Book for Girls (1947)
The Second Chalet Book for Girls (1948)
The Third Chalet Book for Girls (1949)
The Chalet Girls' Cook Book (1953)

COMPLETE NUMERICAL LIST OF TITLES IN THE CHALET SCHOOL SERIES
(Armada/Collins)

1. *The School at the Chalet*
2. *Jo of the Chalet School*
3. *The Princess of the Chalet School*
4. *The Head Girl of the Chalet School*
5. *(The) Rivals of the Chalet School*
6. *Eustacia Goes to the Chalet School*
7. *The Chalet School and Jo*
8. *The Chalet Girls in Camp*
9. *The Exploits of the Chalet Girls*
10. *The Chalet School and the Lintons*
11. *A Rebel at the Chalet School*
12. *The New House at the Chalet School*
13. *Jo Returns to the Chalet School*
14. *The New Chalet School*
15. *A United Chalet School*
16. *The Chalet School in Exile*
17. *The Chalet School at War*
18. *The Highland Twins at the Chalet School*
19. *Lavender Leigh at the Chalet School*
20. *Gay Lambert at the Chalet School*
21. *Jo to the Rescue*
21a. *The Mystery at the Chalet School* (published only in the same volume as 23)
22. *Tom Tackles the Chalet School*
23. *The Chalet School and Rosalie*
24. *Three Go to the Chalet School*
25. *The Chalet School and the Island*
26. *Peggy of the Chalet School*
27. *Carola Storms the Chalet School*
28. *The Wrong Chalet School*

29. *Shocks for the Chalet School*
30. *The Chalet School in the Oberland*
31. *Bride Leads the Chalet School*
32. *Changes for the Chalet School*
33. *Joey Goes to the Oberland*
34. *The Chalet School and Barbara*
35. *The Chalet School Does It Again*
36. *A Chalet Girl from Kenya*
37. *Mary-Lou of the Chalet School*
38. *A Genius at the Chalet School*
39. *Chalet School Fête*
40. *A Problem for the Chalet School*
41. *The New Mistress at the Chalet School*
42. *Excitements at the Chalet School*
43. *The Coming of Age of the Chalet School*
44. *The Chalet School and Richenda*
45. *Trials for the Chalet School*
46. *Theodora and the Chalet School*
47. *Joey and Co. in Tirol*
48. *Ruey Richardson at the Chalet School*
49. *A Leader in the Chalet School*
50. *The Chalet School Wins the Trick*
51. *A Future Chalet School Girl*
52. *The Feud in the Chalet School*
53. *The Chalet School Triplets*
54. *The Chalet School Reunion*
55. *Jane and the Chalet School*
56. *Redheads at the Chalet School*
57. *Adrienne and the Chalet School*
58. *Summer Term at the Chalet School*
59. *Challenge for the Chalet School*
60. *Two Sams at the Chalet School*
61. *Althea Joins the Chalet School*
62. *Prefects of the Chalet School*

NEW CHALET SCHOOL TITLES

In the last few years several authors have written books which either fill in terms in the Chalet School canon about which Elinor did not write or carry on the story. These are as follows:

The Chalet School Christmas Story Book edited by Ruth Jolly and Adrianne Fitzpatrick—featuring short stories by Helen Barber, Katherine Bruce, Caroline German, Heather Paisley and more (Girls Gone By Publishers 2007)

The Bettanys of Taverton High by Helen Barber—set immediately before *The School at the Chalet*, covering Joey's last term at her English school (Girls Gone By Publishers 2008)

The Guides of the Chalet School by Jane Berry—set in the summer term immediately after *Jo of the Chalet School* (Girls Gone By Publishers 2009)

Juliet of the Chalet School by Caroline German—set in the gap between *Jo of the Chalet School* and *The Princess of the Chalet School*, following *The Guides of the Chalet School* (Girls Gone By Publishers 2006; out of print)

Visitors for the Chalet School by Helen McClelland—set between *The Princess of the Chalet School* and *The Head Girl of the Chalet School* (Bettany Press 1995; Collins edition 2000)

Gillian of the Chalet School by Carol Allan—set between *The New Chalet School* and *The Chalet School in Exile* (Girls Gone By Publishers 2001; reprinted 2006; out of print)

The Chalet School and Robin by Caroline German—set after *The Chalet School Goes to It* (Girls Gone By Publishers 2003; out of print)

A Chalet School Headmistress by Helen Barber—set during the same term as *The Mystery at the Chalet School* (Girls Gone By Publishers 2004; out of print)

Peace Comes to the Chalet School by Katherine Bruce—set in the gap between *The Chalet School and Rosalie* and *Three Go to the Chalet School*; the action takes place during the summer term of 1945 (Girls Gone By Publishers 2005; out of print)

New Beginnings at the Chalet School by Heather Paisley—set three years after *Prefects of the Chalet School* (Friends of the Chalet School 1999; Girls Gone By Publishers 2002; reprinted 2006; out of print)

FURTHER READING

Behind the Chalet School by Helen McClelland (essential)*

Elinor M. Brent-Dyer's Chalet School by Helen McClelland. Out of print

The Chalet School Companion by Helen McClelland*

A World of Girls by Rosemary Auchmuty*

A World of Women by Rosemary Auchmuty*

*Available from:
Bettany Press, 8 Kildare Road, London E16 4AD, UK
(http://www.bettanypress.co.uk)

Girls Gone By Publishers, or any of their authors or contributors, have no responsibility for the persistence of accuracy of URLs for external or third-party internet websites referred to in this book, and do not guarantee that any content on such websites is, or will remain, accurate or appropriate.

INDEX OF RECIPES

Almond Icing	127	Cabbage	77	Chips 73
Apple Charlotte . . .	95	Cake		Chocolate 166
Apple Pudding	106	Heidelberg . . .	122	Chop Suey—Chinese . . 65
Apple Tart	92	Sand	124	Chops, Lamb 55
Avignon Tomatoes . . .	80	Twelfth Day . . .	125	Coffee 165
		Cakes: Foundation Recipe .	118	Coffee, Egg 181
Bacon Rasher, grilled . .	55	Caledonian Cream . . .	110	Cream Cheese 146
Baked Custard	99	Caramels, Russian . . .	134	Cream
Baked Stuffed Tomatoes .	84	Cauliflower Soup . . .	29	Caledonian 110
Béchamel Sauce	43	Charlotte, Apple . . .	95	Cucumber 76
Beef, Roast	57	Cheese		Creams, Potato . . . 75
Beef Tea	180	Cream	146	Creamy Rice Pudding . . 100
Billy Tea	164	Macaroni . . .	144	Cucumber Cream . . . 76
Biscuits	130	Cheese Casserole . . .	149	Curry, Madras . . . 66
Blackberry Fluff . . .	107	Cheese Sauce . . .	141	Custard
Boiled Custard	96	Cheese Straws . . .	148	Baked 99
Bortch Soup	35	Chicken, Roast . . .	61	Boiled 96
Butterscotch	133	Chicken Soup . . .	181	

225

Dates, Stuffed 136

Egg Coffee 181
Eggs
Scalloped 157
Scotch 157
Tomato Scrambled . . 83
Everyday Soup 28

Figs, Stuffed 136
Fondant 135
Fondant Sweets
Peppermint Creams . 136
Stuffed Dates . . . 136
Stuffed Figs . . . 136
Stuffed French Prunes . 136
French Omelette 156
French Prunes, Stuffed . . 136
Fudge 137

Gingerbread 119
Goose, Roast 62
Goulash, Hungarian . . . 63
Gravy 57

Haddock, Stuffed Baked . 42
Heidelberg Cake 122
Herbs 177
Hungarian Goulash . . . 63
Hot Pot, Lancashire . . . 64

Icing
Almond 127
for Gingerbread . . 121
Royal 128
Water 124

Julep, Mint 168

Kedgeree 48
Kidney, grilled 55
Kippers
Poached 45
Scrambled 45

Lamb Chops 55
Lamb, Roman Roast . . 60
Lancashire Hot Pot . . . 64
Lemon Syrup 167
Lobster Cutlets 43
Lotus Flower Tomatoes . . 81
Love Dreams 146

Madras Curry 66
Mashed Potatoes 73
Mint Julep 168
Mokka-Jokka 110
Mushrooms on Toast . . 85
Mutton, Roast 57

Neapolitan Macaroni Cheese 144
New Potatoes 72

Omelette, French 156

Pancakes 101
Parsnip Pie 79

INDEX OF RECIPES

Pastry, Short	91
Pea Soup	33
Pears and Chocolate Sauce	108
Peas	77
French Method	78
Poached Eggs	154
Poached Kippers	45
Pork, Roast	57
Potato Creams	75
Potato Soup	28
Potatoes	
Chips	73
Mashed	73
New	72
Puff-Talloons	74
Roast	73
Prunes, French, Stuffed	136
Pudding	
Apple	106
Rice	100
Steamed	103
Suet	105
Puff-Talloons	74
Quinces & Baked Oranges	108
Raspberry Wine	168
Rice	
Fried	50
Indian method	49
Pudding	100
Spanish	143
Roast	
Beef	57
Chicken	61
Goose	62
Lamb, Roman	60
Mutton	57
Pork	57
Potatoes	73
Veal	57
Roman Roast Lamb	60
Royal Icing	128
Rump Steak	55
Russian Caramels	134
Sand Cake	124
Sauce	
Béchamel	43
Cheese	141
Scalloped Eggs	157
Scones	129
Scotch Broth	30
Scotch Eggs	157
Scrambled Kippers	45
Shepherd's Pie	67
Short Pastry	91
Sicilian Sandwich	144
Soup	
Bortch	35
Cauliflower	29
Chicken	181
Everyday	28
Pea	33
Potato	28
Spinach	31
Tomato	32
Spanish Rice	143

Spinach	. . . . .	77
Spinach Soup	. . . .	31
Steak, Rump	. . . . .	55
Steamed Puddings:		
Foundation Recipe	.	103
Stockpot	. . . . .	26
Stuffed Baked Haddock	.	42
Suet Pudding	. . . .	105
Syrup, Lemon	. . . .	167
Tart, Apple	. . . . .	92
Tea .	. . . . .	163
Beef	. . . . .	180
Billy	. . . . .	164
Tomatoes		
Avignon .	. . . .	80
Baked Stuffed	. . .	84
Lotus Flower	. . .	81
Venetian Ladies	. .	82
Tomato Scrambled Eggs	.	83
Tomato Soup .	. . . .	32
Twelfth Day Cake	. . .	125

Veal Roast	. . . . .	57
Vegetable Surprise	. . .	87
Venetian Ladies	. . . .	82
Water Icing	. . . . .	124
Welsh Rarebit	. . . .	143
Wiener Schnitzel	. . .	58
Wine, Raspberry	. . .	168

Girls Gone By Publishers

Girls Gone By Publishers republish some of the most popular children's fiction from the 20th century, concentrating on those titles which are most sought after and difficult to find on the second-hand market. Our aim is to make them available at affordable prices, and to make ownership possible not only for existing collectors but also for new collectors so that the books continue to survive. We also publish some new titles which fit into this genre.

Authors on the GGBP fiction list include Angela Brazil, Margaret Biggs, Elinor Brent-Dyer, Dorita Fairlie Bruce, Christine Chaundler, Gwendoline Courtney, Winifred Darch, Monica Edwards, Josephine Elder, Antonia Forest, Lorna Hill, Clare Mallory, Helen McClelland, Dorothea Moore, Violet Needham, Elsie Jeanette Oxenham, Malcolm Saville, Evelyn Smith and Geoffrey Trease.

We also have a growing range of non-fiction titles, either more general works about the genre or books about particular authors. Our non-fiction authors include Mary Cadogan, James Mackenzie, Brian Parks and Stella Waring and Sheila Ray. These are in a larger format than our fiction titles, and most of them are lavishly illustrated in colour as well as black and white.

For details of availability and when to order (please do not order books until they are actually listed) see our website—www.ggbp.co.uk—or write for a catalogue to Clarissa Cridland or Ann Mackie-Hunter, GGBP, 4 Rock Terrace, Coleford, Bath, BA3 5NF, UK.